THE VENTURE

OF

RATIONAL FAITH

MACMILLAN AND CO., Limited
LONDON · BOMBAY · CALCUTTA
MELBOURNE

THE MACMILLAN COMPANY
NEW YORK · BOSTON · CHICAGO
ATLANTA · SAN FRANCISCO

THE MACMILLAN CO. OF CANADA, Ltd.
TORONTO

THE VENTURE

OF

RATIONAL FAITH

BY

MARGARET BENSON

MACMILLAN AND CO., LIMITED
ST. MARTIN'S STREET, LONDON
1908

PREFACE

FIFTEEN years ago I began to write a book of Christian apologetics, intending, with the sanguine impulse of my age, to meet and answer the historical, scientific, and philosophic difficulties in the way of belief. The first difficulty which met me was the necessity of knowing something about these subjects.

Thus life destroys many of our hopeful anticipations, but even in soberer middle age the germ of the intention is still alive, for Christianity makes no claim to be the religion of the expert only ; it cannot be necessary, if Christianity is in any way what it professes to be, to wait until historical criticism has uttered its last word, or science tried its last experiment, before trusting to the truth of sayings whose authenticity is questioned, or to the power of a life whose uniqueness is challenged.

Yet merely to refer those who make such a

v

plea to "faith" as opposed to "reason" would be a superficial solution of the problem. Reason means no more than logic and faith no more than instinct, if they are mutually exclusive. We are rightly not content to be relegated to the guidance of instinct only in the practical concerns of life, why then should we be content in that which concerns us most deeply, our religious belief?

The aim of this book then is to show the reason of faith, not necessarily to find out a new reason, but to make clear if possible an implicit reason. And those to whom it is addressed are neither the experts on one side, nor on the other those who live by instinct, but average people of educated intelligence. The claim to be average is not an arrogant claim, like the claim to be the plain man, or the man in the street. The plain man insists on being plain; the man in the street rollicks down the street and looks at himself in the plate-glass windows.[1] But none of us wants to be average. That we are so is a melancholy fact borne in upon us in middle life, and we do not always relish it. But at any rate good sense is expected of average people; and those among them who are continually meeting certain

[1] Cf. *God and my Neighbour*, by Robert Blatchford.

"obstinate questionings," while realising that they cannot answer them in a comprehensive fashion upon purely intellectual grounds, must yet claim for their religion some reasonable basis.

What I have therefore attempted to do is not to meet and solve difficulties—for the solution of a difficulty is a matter for the expert—but while recording difficulties to examine the basis on which belief actually rests or may rest, in order to find what reason is implied in it. Then having reached this point to turn round and see what proportion in view of the reason for faith, the reasons for doubt seem to have assumed.

If we have gained a standing-ground on some shore is the tide-mark above or below us? Though we see the waves lapping at our feet, rising, threatening, are we secure within that invisible barrier which holds back the waters?

In every province into which faith enters, not only in the belief in God, but the trust in our friends and in our own business in life, when once standing-ground has been attained, difficulties which threatened break like waves on a rock and are given back in vapour to the air.

But the power of popular doubts can hardly be compared to the strength of waters; they are mists of doubt, phantoms of cross lights and shadows which gain their force only from the lightness or the cowardice which arrests enquiry. Reasonless as much of our faith often is, the popular difficulties which assail it are yet more irrational; least reasonable of all is the position of those who will study neither the difficulties of faith nor the grounds of belief, but let a vague faith be assailed by a yet vaguer doubt, and hardly wait to fight with shadows before they fall or flee.

The simplest touch of reality may dispel such doubt. I once encountered a nursery-maid who rejoiced in grave suspicions of the Pentateuch on the ground that Moses could not write; the sight of an Egyptian eighteenth-dynasty scarab quite unreasonably dispelled a groundless doubt. A voyage to the Holy Land and the apprehension of its geographical reality similarly restored a young sailor to a complete belief in the historical character of all events alleged to have happened there, and he exhorted his mother not to follow his earlier example of disbelief in the curate's sermons. The cause of this is not far to seek, nor does it affect the uneducated only; we cannot believe in anything however true, which has no connection with what we know to be real.

The most fruitful cause of unbelief is not that faith conflicts with what we have learnt to be true, but that it seems to have no connection with what we know to be real, and thus many avoidable as well as unavoidable defects of education have their part in weakening faith. It is unavoidable that we should be taught some fundamental religious doctrines before we have enough experience of life to be capable of testing them; but we are often unnecessarily taught the historical side of our religion apart from its historical setting; not as if it was an integral part of the world's history, with contemporary events and historical antecedents, but as if the events had taken place in a little world apart from our own, in that small alien universe where the sailor had no doubt located the land of Israel side by side with the Garden of Eden. If historical and scientific difficulties are presented to a mind thus nurtured, religious belief is apt to give way for it is felt to be unreal; whereas the objections to it involve facts of that real world of science and history which touches our daily life.

Moreover minds so developed are more open to suspicion than to study. " There is no reason," such an one might argue, " for teaching me the geography of South America, except that it happens to exist; but I might have been taught the doctrine of the resurrection of the dead and final judgment to keep me happy and straight in this life even if no one were sure they were true." Thus the extreme importance of belief becomes a reason against acceptance to an honest mind. Indeed the best counteractive to the secularisation of education would be the secularisation of religion——its connection with the world and with life.

For it is not education only which affects the reality of religion; the positive reasons for belief must be found somehow in the hold on life, and as life grows easier to the educated class (where ideas, beliefs, and doubts take their rise and flow down to the less educated), they are apt to lose some hold on reality. "All things are lawful," and recreation is certainly expedient, but it needs a very profound mind not to lose some sense of reality when attention is much centred on a golf-ball. It is an old truth that the harder realities of life, restoring, as they do, a sense of proportion, bring back religion.

> Almost every one, when age,
> Disease or sorrow strike him,
> Inclines to think there *is* a God
> Or something very like Him.

I will not pretend to examine religious belief with an "unbiassed" mind. If any one is able to look even on his father and mother with an "unbiassed" mind, it argues less the brilliancy of his intellect than the deficiency of his sonship. A "bias" here would be both the cause and the result of truer perception. Still more impossible is it to look "unbiassed" on one's own faith. We cannot divest ourselves of faith like a dress and put it upon a stand for inspection. If we believe in a gospel at all, we believe in a power which has made us what we are and will mould us to what we shall be ; we believe in something which intellect can only try to apprehend in a glass darkly, but which we know to be the core and heart of our life.

But if one cannot be unbiassed one is bound to be fair ; the bias must not allow us to close our eyes to difficulties or to determine a question by a foregone conclusion. Above all, we must remember that our own conviction is not in itself a reason for another person's belief.

On the other hand, the attitude of the enquirer or the sceptic is essentially unbiassed, so we may claim that he also should never arrest the course of reasoning by an *a priori* conclusion ; and that he should endeavour so to apprehend any rational position as to see what belief its reasonableness implies.

The book naturally divides itself into four parts :—

First, an Introduction, dealing with the nature of reasonable belief in general, and showing the failure of the *a priori* argument against the possibility of religion.

Secondly, an examination of the chief difficulties in the way of belief in Christianity.

Thirdly, an examination of the reasons for faith which is implied in any reality of rational life.

The *last part* deals with the comparison of the position thus reached with the main standpoint of Christianity, and the *Epilogue* aims at showing the possible realisation in Christian faith of the conditions of reasonable belief in general.

This book does not pretend to any originality of thought; if there are fewer references to authorities than might have been expected it is for one of two reasons. As this attempt has lasted over a considerable space of time, many ideas which one has derived from books or from people have passed unconsciously into one's own thought; and further, most of the ideas are

common property which can be assigned to no
one author. Thus my only excuse for writing
must be the attempt to take, from the inside, a
comprehensive view of the position of the average
person, to see its necessary limitations as well as
its possibilities in the way of knowledge and
experience, and to decide how far, in these circumstances, a rational life involves a reasonable
faith.

MARGARET BENSON.

1907.

[The author having been prevented by recent
severe illness from correcting the proofs of this
book, I have, at her request, seen it through the
press; thus it has not had the advantage of her
own final supervision. Sincerest thanks are due
to those who have given valuable help in revision
and verification.

JANET GOURLAY.]

1908.

CONTENTS

PART I.—INTRODUCTORY

PAGE

CHAP. I.—THE CONDITIONS AND NATURE OF REASON-
ABLE BELIEF 3

§ 1. Fundamental principles of thought. § 2. Beliefs received on authority. § 3. Principles of practical action.
§ 4. Irresistible conviction. § 5. Knowledge derived from
(a) simple, (b) scientific experience. § 6. Verification.
§ 7. Analogical religious beliefs. § 8. Relation of religious
belief to belief in general.

CHAP. II.—THE IMPOSSIBILITY OF PHILOSOPHIC MATER-
IALISM 20

§ 1. Scientific materialism. § 2. Philosophic consideration of scientific terms. § 3. Ethereal forms of materialism.

PART II.—CRITICAL

A.—THE DIFFICULTIES OF SCIENCE

CHAP. I.—DEFINITION OF SCIENTIFIC DIFFICULTIES . 39

§ 1. The relation of God to the world. § 2. Different
aspects of religion and science.

PAGE

CHAP. II.—SCIENCE AND MIRACLES   49

§ 1. Divine action through known law.   § 2. Divine
action through unknown law.   § 3.   Divine action in
"contradiction to known law."   § 4. Divine providence
through all events.

CHAP. III.—SCIENCE AND MIRACLES   58

§ 1. Meaning of "opposition."   § 2. Absence of continuity of causation.   § 3. Arbitrary and unique events.
§ 4. Connection of ideal and material.   § 5. Connection
of divine idea with the material.

CHAP. IV.—SCIENCE AND PERSONALITY   .   .   .   67

§ 1. Personality and law.   § 2. Scientific conclusions
and rational belief.

B.—THE UNCERTAINTIES OF HISTORY

CHAP. V.—THE RECORDS OF CHRISTIANITY.   .   .   77

Definition of uncertainties.

CHAP. VI.—SCIENTIFIC ACCURACY AND ARTISTIC TRUTH   84

§ 1. Contrast of attitude.   § 2. The aspect of the historian.

CHAP. VII.—EVIDENCE FROM RECORDS   .   .   .   95

§ 1. Suitability of evidence.   § 2. St. Paul's evidence.
§ 3. The synoptic gospels.   § 4. The Fourth Gospel.   § 5.
Other evidence.

CHAP. VIII.—ESTIMATION OF EVIDENCE   .   .   .   120

§ 1. The complexity of personality.   § 2. The idealising
tendency.   § 3. Summary of the question.

PAGE

CHAP. IX.—(TRANSITION TO *C.*) THE GENESIS OF
RELIGIOUS IDEAS 136

Relation of evidence from records to evidence of results.
Christianity and natural religion.

C.—PARALLELISM OF CHRISTIANITY AND OTHER
RELIGIONS

CHAP. X.—RESEMBLANCES OF DOCTRINES, RITES, NAR-
RATIVES 142

CHAP. XI.—EVOLUTION OF RELIGIOUS IDEAS . . 154

CHAP. XII.—EVOLUTION AND REVELATION . . . 161

CHAP. XIII.—TRANSITION TO PART III. . . . 168

§ 1. Review of scientific and historic difficulties. § 2.
Popular solution. § 3. Necessity of special evidence.

PART III.—CONSTRUCTIVE

CHAP. I.—INTRODUCTORY—THE NATURE OF POSITIVE
EVIDENCE 179

A.—THE MORAL DEMAND

CHAP. II.—THE MORAL IDEAL AND MORAL OBLIGATION 184

CHAP. III.—ARGUMENT FROM ACTUAL IMPERFECTION . 190

§ 1. Sin and suffering. § 2. Time and the end. § 3.
The object of philosophy.

PAGE

CHAP. IV.—EXISTENCES IMPLIED IN MORALITY .   . 209

§ 1. Wisdom in the universe.   § 2. Objection—The
evolution of morality.   § 3. The belief in spiritual power.
§ 4. The necessity of redemptive action.   § 5. Choice as
an element in rational belief.

B.—THE SPIRITUAL REALITIES

CHAP. V.—TESTS OF SPIRITUAL EXPERIENCE   .   . 225

§ 1. Experience, delusion, mistake.   § 2. The correspondence to moral demand.   § 3. Spiritual experience
and ethical experience.

CHAP. VI.—EVIDENCE OF SPIRITUAL REALITIES .   . 238

§ 1. Conversion and its interpretation.   § 2. Thought,
emotion, perception—only forms of manifestation.   § 3.
Rationality of belief in spiritual power.   § 4. Power and
personality.

PART IV.—THE MYSTERY OF PERSONALITY

A.—VERIFICATION OF PRINCIPLES IMPLIED
IN HIGHER EXPERIENCES

CHAP. I.   253

§ 1. Actual and ideal world.   § 2. Verification by historic
manifestation.   § 3. Unity of Christian doctrines and
ethics.

B.—EXAMINATION OF THREE FUNDAMENTAL
CHRISTIAN DOCTRINES

CHAP. II.—THE FATHERHOOD OF GOD   .   .   . 264

§ 1. The idea of Providence.   § 2. The doctrine of
" adoption."   § 3. Revelation through the Son.

CONTENTS

PAGE

CHAP. III.—THE REDEMPTION THROUGH THE SON . 274

§ 1. Metaphor in religion. § 2. Sacrifice in nature, life, and rite. § 3. Conditions of redemptive sacrifice. § 4. Communion and will-sacrifice. § 5. Propitiation.

CHAP. IV.—THE SPIRIT IN THE CHURCH . . . 297

§ 1. Social relation of the spiritual being. § 2. The spiritual community. § 3. The Christian Church.

C.—CONCLUSION

CHAP. V.—THE VENTURE OF RATIONAL FAITH . . 307

§ 1. Christianity and personality. § 2. The inadequacy of difficulties.

EPILOGUE

THE CONDITIONS OF REASONABLE BELIEF IN RELATION TO FAITH 313

PART I

INTRODUCTORY

B

CHAPTER I

THE CONDITIONS AND NATURE OF REASONABLE
BELIEF

§ 1. BEFORE we are in a position to judge
whether our religious beliefs are reasonable, it is
evident that we must first form some idea of the
nature of reasonable belief in general.

We often speak as if we could only hold a
rational belief about matters which we had tested
by such proofs as would seem conclusive to the
scientific man or the lawyer; but reflection will
show that the things we believe on well-tested
evidence form a very small part of the things
which we may, indeed which we must, believe
if we are to live like rational beings in the
world. For if we want to consider rational
belief in its largest sense, we must include the
principles which guide our action rightly and
help us to extend our knowledge. We must
include therefore, not only those beliefs which
are tested by reason, but those that are in
accordance with it or serviceable to it. Let us

begin by distinguishing five possible kinds of
rational belief.

In the first class we include the principles of
thought which are implied in perception and
processes of reasoning : such principles are prior
to evidence because they are implied in the very
existence of evidence.   Even in observation
some principles and arrangement of thought are
necessary, otherwise impressions would flash upon
our eye and ear and vanish, timeless, formless,
orderless, as we can imagine they must slide unnoticed across the mind of an imbecile.   Further
principles are implied in all our reasoning ; and the
whole structure of science rests upon the assumption that every event has a cause, and that the
same cause always produces the same effect.
Yet this fundamental principle on which all
scientific reasoning is based, cannot be logically
proved.   We may indeed have arrived at the
Law of Causation through the association of
cause and effect in simple cases : we are not long
in discovering that fire always burns and water
invariably wets, and our sensations in such cases
do not allow us to forget the result.   But simple
association is not proof; and in complicated
instances we are continually confronted with cases
in which things happen without an apparent
cause, or in which the same cause does not seem
to produce the same effect.   We are all familiar
with the experiments of youthful students of

chemistry, where everything was done right and the wrong result followed ; or the domestic experience of housemaids, who took up the china as they had always done, and it " flew to pieces in their hands." Thus we cannot prove the uniformity of nature by invariable experience of uniformity ; and every other method of logical proof implies that we already believe in it.

The only true proof of the uniformity of nature is that whenever we take for granted that it is true, it ultimately proves itself to be so ; for it is the re-assertion of this discriminating principle which enables us again to corroborate it in the face of contradictory experience, which induces the operator to repeat his experiment more carefully, and persuades the housemaid that some unnoticed circumstance must have induced the plate "to fly." It is this which, when a planet persistently refuses to obey the law of gravitation, directs the telescope to the path of its new lord or unseen master ; and through all apparent contradiction the course of experience will testify again and again to the truth of its fundamental and formative principle — the Uniformity of Nature. But it will only confirm the faith we have held through apparent contradiction, and only confirm it because we have held it.

If this is true with regard to our scientific beliefs, it is possible that we may find something analogous in the case of religious beliefs ; that some part of our religious beliefs may consist of

fundamental principles without which we could
have no religious experience.

Thus it has always been urged by those who
believe in the love of God that this belief forms
and moulds all spiritual experience; that it cannot
be proved by purely external observation, for he
who does not believe in it lacks the discriminating element in observation and the transforming
element in experience; but that the man who
holds it in the face of apparent contradiction
finds these contradictions but the road to new
laws and new truth, and discovers that the evil
chances of this life open to his vision new depths
of God's love.

If such an argument appears to be illogical in
religious matters, we must remember that the
whole basis of our science is illogical in the same
way.

§ 2. But if any one will examine himself, he
will find that by far the greater part of the
knowledge which he calls his own rests upon
authority.

What do most educated people know about
history or about science ?

The greater part of our education implies that
we know a little of *what has been said* about a
subject; we accept our history, and our science
we take on the authority of others. And the
background to our knowledge is a sense of the
general agreement of opinion.

This is quite a sound basis in reality, but it is plain that evidence is not here the foundation of our belief, but only one test of it. Now and then we handle a historic monument which others indeed must interpret for us ; here and there we confirm our scientific principles by a domestic experiment. We know the power of a vacuum as shown in the common pump, though we vaguely understand its mechanism ; we know the electric bells ring when the man has put them right. Yet the conviction of the truth of science is none the less sure because it consists in the link between the vague feeling of the general consensus of opinion and the tag end of reality held in our hands, which converts by magic touch the theory into conviction. The electric bell *does* ring, the common pump *is* working in the yard.

All this indeed stretches far beyond us, but it also comes close to us ; the backgrounds of our various "subjects" seem harmonious ; the pump man for instance has no scientific quarrel with the electric bell man. Thus, until we begin to examine the foundation of belief, it does not occur to us that the grounds of such knowledge do not really rest on evidence tested by ourselves at all. Yet the man who rejected this body of knowledge because he was not able to test it would not be the more rational but the less rational man. Even those who by careful sifting of evidence add to knowledge must first take their stand on authority ; and the scientific expert

himself can test but a small part of the knowledge which forms the basis for his original
research; his very discoveries are based on what
he has received on authority. The whole body
of knowledge indeed is a corporate possession of
which the individual can assimilate but a small
part.

It may be said that all progress in knowledge
takes place through the correction of that which
has been received on authority, and this is true; but
without the huge body of traditional knowledge,
accurate and inaccurate together, there would be
nothing even to correct. Progress is not made
in spite of authority, but by means of it.

If, then, the largest part of our rational beliefs
in general rests on authority, there is no *a priori*
reason why our religious beliefs should not rest
on authority.

But here we should be met by the objection
that there is not a general consensus of opinion in
religious matters. We can only comment briefly
on the objection here and point out that the
difference between the two cases may easily be
exaggerated: the savage races of the world probably agree quite as little with our science as with
our religion; and when we speak of the general consensus of opinion, we mean merely the consensus
of the most expert opinion, and the possibility
of thereby convincing any sufficiently intelligent
disciple. But even the consensus of educated
opinion in science has sometimes been proved to

be opposed to the truth.   Galileo has been *contra mundum* as well as Athanasius.   We are slower to recognise the place of the expert in religion, and indeed in this region he is usually called a *fanatic* ; but it would be difficult to support the position that here alone attention to the subject is a disadvantage.   Moreover we are not cut off from testing in our own experience the religious truths which we receive on authority, exactly as we test the scientific truths.   It is sometimes forgotten that this test alone can give reality to our beliefs in either case.

§ 3. In the third place, our practical actions imply certain principles of which we only become conscious by analysis ; but in so far as these principles lead us to correct conclusions and rational actions, we must call them, in the largest sense, rational beliefs.

The observation of animals helps to show us how we may act on such rational principles before they have emerged into full consciousness.   We have some common octaves of thought with many animals, we have the same keynote ; their intellect, conscious and instinctive, is based on the same uniformity of nature more dimly discerned.

The robin who follows in summer some quite alien being, noticing the voice and look which distinguish his human friend from his animal foes, and who day by day in winter seeks food from the same friend, is guided by the same rational principle as that which underlies all our scientific systems—namely, the principle of uniformity. Yet much of his rational action is unconscious, for the dim workings of his reason will not serve to explain all the manifold adjustments of his actions to his surrounding world, whereby the nest is prepared for the eggs and the young are sheltered and fed, or even the simpler actions involved in the search for food, or in self-defence. We see that the rational principles which guide his action have their root in his physical nature. The physical constitution, with its punctual recurrent appetites which find their satisfaction in the material things of the world; emotions, impulses which have their outcome in life and the reproduction of life; the imitative instinct, association, with its distincter sister, memory— all these form the great foundation of the universal reason, out of which emerges the individual understanding. But these underlying principles of practical action must come into full consciousness before they can be evidentially tested, and until then such beliefs are to be considered rather as the product of causes than as the conclusions of the understanding. They are rational, however, if they are in harmony with reason even though they are not the result of logical reasoning.

This brings us to a further fact of great importance in the region of human action—namely, that belief may even create its own evidence.

We have not to deal with a world fixed and finished, but with a world which is in the process of becoming. Let us go back to our example. The robin associates a certain figure and voice with his daily bread ; he is right. But certainly the immediate cause of the provision of that bread is the robin's belief; for if I did not see him expectant and ruffled at my feet, I should not go back to the house for it. His need compels me in the main, but his belief upon the instant ; thus his belief creates in part its own evidence.

Thus if we press the question of evidence in too critical a spirit, we sometimes destroy the very matter of evidence by destroying the belief which is a factor in its production ; if we would see certain vital forces at work, there is a point where even vivisection must stay its hand. Too critical a habit with regard to the action of our friends is apt to destroy not only sympathetic insight, but the very ability of the friend to display certain qualities of character. Too much circumspection even about our motives and feelings will actually enfeeble our motives, render our emotions morbid and our actions vacillating. It is scientifically true sometimes that " I caused the change that I foretold," and that I caused it by foretelling it.

If, then, in the region of religion we find that, underlying our practical action, there are principles and beliefs which have their root in the non-rational part of our nature, our emotions, our needs, we should not therefore call them irrational. If we find that an attitude of belief is necessary to the observation of certain vital religious truths, we shall remember that the same attitude is necessary to the observation of other vital truths. If we find that faith can call into actuality that in which it believes, we shall remember that this is paralleled in the common facts of daily life.

§ 4. Further, we must distinguish what is called "immediate conviction," of which we can say little. The term is often wrongly used, for people say they have an immediate conviction when they have really made a rapid inference. If a conviction is really immediate it must be the conviction of something within one's actual consciousness. That there is, external to oneself, grass which is green, is an inference ; that I have a perception of green grass is an immediate conviction. So though the existence of an external world may be an inference, it is conceivable that the contact of spirit with spirit may be a matter of immediate conviction.

§ 5. Finally, we come to (a) the small mass of knowledge which we have gained for ourselves from among the things we have observed. The worth of this kind of knowledge depends almost entirely on the habits of mind, the previous education, the nearness or remoteness of the field of study.

Much that we call observation has no relation to evidence because it involves no discrimination ; but yet persons of any shrewdness will somehow collect during a lifetime a large mass of knowledge drawn from observation which is sufficiently true to be useful.   Many drugs, for instance, are but certificated herbalist remedies.   Such observation has produced the proverbial truths and the shrewd knowledge of conduct or character which makes men pleasant or effective in the world of human action.

And we have also (*b*) the knowledge which we ourselves have tested scientifically.   But even though this is what we call an age of specialisation, this part of knowledge forms a very small proportion of the whole sum of the knowledge of any individual.

§ 6. About the whole body of knowledge thus tested—science in all its branches—we need say nothing : its claims are continually before us, and on the whole we are far too prone to speak as if we could not rationally believe in any other kind of knowledge.   Yet all our knowledge is capable of some kind of verification, and we often do not perceive this because we seek for verification in the wrong region and for evidence of the wrong kind.

" I have swept the heavens with my telescope and have not found God," said Laplace.   As well might a blind man say, " I have listened day and night and have not heard scarlet." The religious man asserts precisely the same truth as Laplace when he confesses

> Nothing like Thyself appears
> Through all these spacious works of Thine ;

but he realises that this confession does not prove his belief irrational.

For faith after all is one faculty of evidence. In mundane matters we know this to be the case, for life is made up not mainly of mechanical forces but of vital forces, for the perception, often for the very existence of which, faith is as necessary as breath for life. We cannot really know our friends except through a faith which not only perceives but kindles latent possibilities and powers.[1]

If we now consider the different kinds of knowledge which we have already enumerated, we shall see that there is some kind of corresponding verification appropriate to each.

(*a*) The fundamental principles of experience can have, as we have seen, no evidential proof, but their verification is found in the fact of their necessity ; for as long as we cling to them the world is rational ; if we were to reject them we should fall into a universal scepticism which is the only completely irrational attitude.

(*b*) Again, in spite of the fact that the false is

---

[1] Your mistress saw your spirit's grace,
When, turning from the ugly face,
    I found belief in it too hard.
                  Easter Day.

mixed with the true in the knowledge which we
receive on authority, it would perhaps be less
rational to reject traditional knowledge than even
to receive it without any test; incredulity is more
often a barrier to the acquisition of truth than a
defence against superstition; and scepticism may
come not from an excess but from a defect of intellect. There is no incredulity like the incredulity
of the ignorant.

Nevertheless we do not really hold a rational
attitude towards traditional knowledge unless we
try to discern the worth of the authority through
which we reach it; until we try to reconcile it
with the rest of our knowledge, and until by committing ourselves to it, we prove that it will bear
the test of reality—only then can we hold it with
conviction. Thus we prove it in homely phrase
by " making it our own."

(c) The beliefs involved in our practical and
rational action find their justification in life. The
right adjustment of our very bodily actions and
needs, nay, the response of the chemical elements
of our being, to external things, form the basis
on which the conscious understanding rests. The
newer psychology is each day showing the greater
importance of the knowledge possessed by the
unconscious self, which includes not only things
once known and apparently forgotten, though
they are still implied in our conscious knowledge, but also the knowledge which has never
yet emerged into consciousness. Yet all such

unconscious beliefs are rational in so far as they are in true relation to the facts of the universe.

Thus we continually respond in a rational manner to things of which we are not conscious; and further, in the higher developments of life we find that we must shape our actions not only in relation to that which actually is or has been, but to that which may be. No man can effectively live among men who will not act on what men may become as well as what they actually are; and faith in possibilities is here a faculty of evidence in the largest sense.

Thus in its lower unconscious working, as in its higher visionary flights, the individual understanding rests upon a reason in the universe; and the rationality of its attitude is evidenced not by the fact that we have proved the reasonableness of our beliefs beforehand, but that through them we live a progressive rational life.

§ 7. Now in the whole consideration of a rational attitude in religion we shall find that there are many different regions of belief as there are many different kinds of knowledge involved.

There are certain fundamental beliefs which are not and cannot be in contradiction to positive science because they are in a wholly different plane.

Our belief in the ultimate purpose of God and the goal to which development tends, is in no kind of contradiction to our belief in the continuous chain of causation which we call evolu-

tion, any more than the fact that a series of
material acts which results in our receiving a
letter from the postman is in contradiction to the
fact that it conveys the message and tells us the
purpose of our friend.

Secondly, unless we received beliefs on authority we should have no opportunity of proving
their truth, we should cut ourselves off from the
stream of religious thought and experience.   To
accept until we can prove is more rational than to
reject.

Again, in religion as in other regions of life,
conscious reason may rest upon a great sub-
stratum of unconscious life—of needs, emotions,
impulses which find through action their true
satisfaction.   The principles which underlie the
action are, while we are still unconscious of them,
rational principles if they are in harmony with
the facts of existence ; if, that is, they find their
true satisfaction, their answer, in their practical
use in life.

Thus it is not so irrational as it appears to
speak of the evidence of the heart or of the feelings ; our practical life is moulded as much by our
feelings in the largest sense as by our understanding, and beliefs underlie these feelings,
beliefs in the making which are gradually formed
and corrected by the understanding.   Our stake
is in life, and it is the necessities of living which
form these beliefs and the exigencies of life which
correct them.

C

Finally, we must ask whether there exists in any one as immediate a conviction of a divine Spirit as that which we have of the existence of human spirit, a conviction which so forces itself upon the mind that 'proof is no longer necessary.

§ 8. But the subject of our investigation is not only religious belief in general, but the Christian religion in particular, and we have to realise that Christianity is not merely a religious theory of the universe, but that it involves a series of definite historic facts ; and that in so far as it does so it comes into the regions of history and science, where strict evidential tests are demanded.

Yet, as we shall see, the historical and the scientific facts involved cannot be considered apart from the fundamental principles of reasonable belief ; and in religion as in other regions of knowledge we may have for a time to accept things that are apparently in contradiction, even as scientific men are obliged for the moment to accept certain features of wireless telegraphy which appear to conflict with known laws.   To reject at once apparently contradictory phenomena would be to stunt the growth of science ; indeed, it is often such apparent contradiction, for example the deflection in the orbit of a planet, which leads to new discoveries.

It is not always unintelligent therefore to accept for the moment the two sides of an apparent contradiction; and the "moment" in the history of the world for which we have to accept it, may be in the history of the individual a long moment—a very lifetime; but to rest contented with the contradiction, to give up aspiring towards a reconciliation, is another thing: this is indeed irrational. The intelligent mind is only stimulated to new effort by apparent contradiction.

The first necessity is to make clear what difficulties we have to face when we compare the events narrated in Christian history with the rest of our historical and scientific knowledge. The first part of this book is devoted to the consideration of this subject.

CHAPTER II

§ 1. BEFORE we proceed to examine the difficulties presented by historical Christianity, we must briefly consider a theory which, if it could be proved, would destroy even the possibility of religion. That theory is the hybrid of philosophy and science which is called Materialism.

If it can be shown that spirit is a mere product of the material universe, there is no God; and therefore there is no need for further enquiry into the reasonableness of religious belief.

It is both impossible and unnecessary here to deal with materialism at any length. The two main standpoints of scientific materialism are very simple: they are the obvious conclusions arrived at by the mind of average intelligence when the attention is directed mainly to the subject of physical science, and no philosophic training is necessary in order to understand them.

Scientific materialism takes its stand on the fact that the material world existed for long ages before life appeared on it; and on the historic

development of rudimentary life into consciousness.   We cannot indeed observe the continuous
evolution of life through different species of living
creatures up to the point where consciousness
begins, but we can observe the development of
the individual consciousness ; for we can trace in
the egg the beginning of organic life which
develops into the bird ; and we see that the
chicken on emerging responds to the external
conditions of life, takes the food and water necessary to sustain it, and comes to the mother's call.
The human being, again, passing through similar
embryonic stages, emerges with less independent
power, but in higher and more complex relation
to the powers that sustain and foster his life, and
after a longer tutelage reaches a higher stage of
consciousness.   It can then be shown that the
evolution of species corresponds to the development of individual life.   We cannot prove, it is
true, that there is only one beginning of organic
life, out of which all kinds of living creatures have
developed ; and it may be the case that life,
originating at various times, under various circumstances, has formed developing centres of
certain great groups of species.   But we know
enough of the course of development to take
for granted without possibility of dispute that
there has been gradual evolution, physically
conditioned, from rudimentary life to conscious
mind.   We have noted a sufficient number of
milestones on the road of evolution to make us

sure that the road does lie continuously between them.

The argument of the materialist then runs briefly thus : In the universe, as science reveals it to us, matter preceded mind. The period during which the earth contained no living plant or creature is immeasurably the longest part of its history. No one knows how life began ; no one can prove whether or no life suddenly appeared as the product of some combination of chemical elements under peculiar conditions.

Our present experience indeed invariably shows us that life is derived from life, and scientific men are unable to discover any conditions in which life begins spontaneously. Yet the impossibility of " spontaneous generation " cannot be proved ; and in the present state of our knowledge we must regard it as an open question.

The whole presupposition and the whole result of science is to show us the continuity of development.[1]

It is of course evident that the preceding argument is not a complete demonstrative argument. Spontaneous generation is admittedly unproved ; the development of the individual, *e.g.*, of the human being, from the rudimentary cell to the rational man could not prove the gradual evolution of mind from species to species, because the

---

[1] This conclusion is not affected, for the purpose of our present argument, by the existence of unexplained instances of "discontinuous variation."

originating cause of the body and mind of the child is obviously not its own early stages of development, but the two developed beings from whom this whole process originates, just as the real cause of the oak is not the acorn but the oak tree.

However it is not on the gaps in the argument that we are inclined to lay stress.   Let us admit that the argument has a strong ground of probability if it confines itself to the scientific region, that is, if it merely presents that continuous chain of causation which we call *evolution*, from the starry nebula to the world of inorganic matter ; from the dead earth of matter to the world of organic life, vegetable and animal ; and finally, the development from the living body to the conscious mind.

But the fact that this chain of causation is continuous does not prove that matter is the originating cause of mind.   How did this matter itself originate ?   We can show no process of evolution by which the nebula itself began ; far less can we show how there originated out of nothing such a nebula as could evolve a mind. Whence do the powers and forces originate, by means of which this nebula proceeds from change to change till consciousness is evolved ?

But let us suppose that the materialist persists with his argument.   " It must be presumed that the cause of life is simply some condition of the inorganic matter which certainly preceded organic life in the history of our world ; and if spontaneous generation is possible, this matter-without-mind did actually produce in the course of evolution matter-with-mind."

Let us grant (for the sake of argument) the utmost that the materialist can demand—spontaneous generation, or a continuous transition from inorganic to organic matter; and again a continuous transition from organic matter to consciousness. Yet is the materialist right in asserting that inorganic matter, *i.e.* matter which does not show *the physical effects of life*, is *matter-without-mind*? Is there any such thing as *matter-without-mind*?

We will return to this main point, only let us first note the confirmatory argument of the materialist : that material changes always accompany mental changes, that external material objects affect the material brain through the material organs of perception, and that such changes are accompanied by what we call ideas ; or, again, that a material change, such as a clot on the brain, or the removal of a certain part of the brain, is followed by a mental change, the loss of an idea or the acquisition of a new idea. From such premises it is concluded that the material changes which are known to accompany mental changes really cause them ; and the establishment of this fact lends a strong confirmation to the preceding argument that matter is the cause of mind. The whole theory is complete, continuous and consistent.

This confirmatory argument which seems so plausible, would be stronger yet if it could be shown that the material changes in the brain precede the mental changes.   But it appears that the actual effect on the material of the brain is synchronous with the idea.   Moreover, though it is indubitable that a material change, a rush of blood to the head, a clot on the brain, a concussion, affects the mental faculties, it is equally clear that the mental faculties affect the material; that hope stimulates the bodily organism; confidence enables it to actually resist and cast out the cells of disease; courage braces it.

But it may be urged again that mental energy is only caused by external conditions, and that though the mind has some little power of reaction against such material conditions, just as a ball thrown at a wall rebounds with what remains to it of the force which sent it, yet that this reactionary power of mind over matter is insignificant compared to the vast material forces of our world, which itself is only an atom in the universe of space.   Let a man note his own tiny power of movement or of life in the grasp of the physical forces within him and around him; note the powers of this world, not only the earthquakes, fire and storm, but the daily tide of day and night, the fundamental forces of light, gravitation, electricity, chemical action and reaction; and then let him look on the stars at night and know that where his puny sight sees stars, even his telescope might give him a glowing, golden disc of light and yet fail to show him a myriadth part of the wonders of space. What remains to him then of the power of his mind—his, the crown of conscious life in the world—even if he could rule seas and storms, even if he could absolutely dominate the particles of his own body or increase his stature by a cubit?

This fact remains, that mind like a creeping tide is coming up over nature on this earth inch by inch, not only by means of the first immediate assimilation and change of inorganic matter under the vital influence — the conversion of earth and water into vegetable and animal life, the instinctive use of the world and its forces by living organisms ; but also by means of the knowledge through which the higher animals and we ourselves convert the laws of the world from our masters into our servants—often rebellious, intractable and destructive, but more and more our servants as we learn to understand them.

We must in fact separate the emotional effect of the contrast between the immensity of material forces and the helplessness of mind from the intellectual weight of the thought. As an intellectual element in the problem, twenty million miles are not more important than twenty yards, and the far-distant constellation towards which our whole solar system is rushing is not something more than material because it is so very far off; it does not more transcend our mental faculties than the pebble at our feet because it gloriously defies our imagination.

But though life is thus gradually transforming the material universe, yet it is possible that the rising tide of life may ebb again ; indeed science seems to show that on this earth it will ebb again, and leave all dark and extinct as the moon.   But it is not really with this flow and ebb of life within the physical sphere that we are concerned.   If all the world became a globe of inorganic matter, the fundamental question would yet remain, Is there such a thing as matter without mind ?

§ 2. What do we mean by matter?   The things we call material are of a certain colour, shape, size, texture, weight, hardness ; but what do all these qualities, what does colour for instance really mean ?   When we say that the grass is green, we mean that in ordinary daylight a person who has normal eyes and a normal brain will receive on looking at the grass a certain sensation which we all agree to call green.   In moonlight, in darkness he will not receive this sensation ; and the sensation a colour-blind person receives from a green leaf is the same as that which he receives from a red geranium ; or, in other words, *he* sees the leaf red.

But it is just the sensation which normal people receive when the light falls in a certain way upon the retina that we mean by green ; green is nothing else than this, it is not an independent thing in itself, but implies a normal organ of vision and a perceptive mind, just as that which we call sound implies a hearing ear and a perceptive mind.

Thus these material qualities imply a mental element.

But it may be said that such fundamental or primary qualities of matter as size, shape, and weight are independent of us; there is nothing that corresponds to "colour-blindness" here; we know the thing *as it is in itself.*

It is quite true that there is no such variation in the sense-organs by which we perceive shape as in the sense of sight, but in speaking of shape we are none the less implying a mental element. What is an angle? There have been people who could not apprehend it, but could only recognise the lines which enclose it, could not see the identity of the angle when the enclosing lines were lengthened. Yet the lines are not the angle. For that which we mean by an angle is in reality an *idea*, the relation between two lines that is recognised by a normal mind.

It is, of course, evident that for the deficient mind, the mindless thing, the angle does not exist; but it is not quite so obvious that we do not really mean anything at all by the angle unless we tacitly presuppose a mind which can apprehend it; for what we mean by space is a relation between points, and "space" therefore implies that which can relate, *i.e.* a mind.

But some one might reply that, although what

we call green does not exist apart from the perceiving and intelligent mind, yet that which *causes*
the eye to see green, the vibration of ether, does
exist independently and has effect on other things
besides ourselves.   In some such sense Mill
defined matter as "a Permanent Possibility of
Sensation."   But "vibration" means movement
in space, and therefore essentially implies relation,
and the very meaning of cause is a relation between things ; not only a relation of things in
time, when one is observed by the perceptive
mind to follow the other, but the actual *production* of one by the other ; cause implies thus a
relation between things which cannot even be
observed.   The idea of causation or production is
supplied by mind ; the uniformity of causation is
re-affirmed by mind whenever it appears to fail.
If we were to take away the mind-element,
"cause" would become meaningless.

But a difficulty which would at once be urged
is the following : *processes* go on continually in
nature, whether or no there is any one to perceive
them.   While the sower sleeps the corn springs
up and ripens.   There may be no mind there to
perceive the corn as green nor to hear its rustle
in the wind, nor any mind to think how it is produced, but the change has gone on and the human
mind has, so to speak, to catch and keep this
matter again, to perceive and understand it at
another point in its independent development.

The difficulty is not without force ; it is

precisely on this ground that Berkeley rested the
proof of the existence of God.   As matter means
nothing apart from mind, yet since matter exists
independently of any created mind, Berkeley concluded that there must be always and everywhere
a perceiving mind.   For the fact of the continuous
development of natural things apart from us in no
way answers the metaphysical difficulty, that we
can attach no meaning to " matter " apart from
mind. What is it ? Without colour, without sound,
without the relations in time and space which
the mind alone can assign to it, without form and
void, it has nothing by which we can describe or
think it.   We are driven in fact, whenever we talk
of matter, tacitly to suppose it as having those
qualities which imply a mental element; to presuppose, that is to say, a perceptive reason.

We cannot, of course, assert that *there is no
other relating* principle in the universe but mind ;
but we cannot help admitting that any idea of
matter in itself apart from mind is wholly *irrational* and unmeaning to us.   If we would
philosophise at all we *cannot* deal with matter in
itself.   We can of course for scientific purposes
abstract our attention from the mental element,
and deal abstractly with matter ; exactly as in
mathematics we abstract attention from the
material thing and deal abstractly with number.
But directly we begin to consider the whole
scheme of things which is the subject of philosophy, directly we begin to consider the real,

CHAP. II   PHILOSOPHIC MATERIALISM   31

fundamental relation of matter and mind, we have
to acknowledge that we cannot even think of
matter as wholly apart from mind.

It seems that it ought to be quite easy to cease
philosophising; but as a matter of fact it is an
almost incorrigible tendency of human nature.
Many a man will start by saying, " I know nothing
beyond the course of this world. In this world
science seems to point to a development from
inorganic to organic, and seems to show a continuity of development from the organic to the
conscious life." But it is a thousand to one that
he will go on to say, first, " I *can* know nothing
beyond the limits of this world "; and secondly,
" My mind is the only instrument for judging
which I have, and *it* can know nothing beyond
the course of this world." Thirdly, he will assert
" *No one* knows anything beyond the course of
this world." In which philosophy he will be
found to have made many assertions beyond the
limit marked out for himself, notably that that
which is beyond the limits of his knowledge is
unknowable not only by himself but by others.

But his safety is not found in ceasing to philosophise (for, as we say, the tendency is probably
ineradicable), but in becoming conscious that he
is doing so; and that therefore he must not make
general statements about " knowledge " without
examining the theory of knowledge, nor build up
a system on ideas which analysis shows to be
meaningless. Such an idea emphatically is the

idea of *matter-without-mind*. No man really knows nor can explain what he means by matter apart from mind. The convenient abstractions of language enable him to talk about it, but once he begins to analyse his thought of it he will find this immanent Mind always present.

To enquire into the various systems of idealism, or the question of whether we must conceive of mind as the originating cause of matter, would be far too large a task for our present purpose. All that we are immediately concerned to establish is that little as we know what mind is, we know still less what matter is : the one thing we are certain of is that mind exists. The real existence of the world external to us is an inference from our own experience, whereas our knowledge of our mental existence is immediate.

The external world consists of "people" and "things"; we infer that they exist in a certain degree of independence from our individual selves.

Science gives us reason to believe that in this world the experiences we call "things" or "matter" are the physical causes of our immediate selves. But when we are tempted to say that matter is therefore the *originating* cause of mind, we have to remember that "matter" is, after all, only one item of mental experience.

When we have accepted this conclusion, we appear at first to have landed ourselves in an individualist position ; we seem to have made our own mind the centre and basis of all things, to have rested all else as an inference on it.   But though we have shown that our mind cannot be simply the product of matter-without-mind, we have not thereby proved that it is self-dependent.

The belief in the existence of minds other than our own may be based, like our belief in things, upon our own experience ; but the *idea* of minds other than our own is not irrational or meaning-less as is the idea of matter apart from any mind, and we may find, as we go on, reason to believe, from an examination of our own mind, that it is not, and cannot be, independent.   As the exist-ence of matter implies the existence of mind, so we may find that the phenomena of our own mind cannot be comprehended if we suppose it to be self-dependent.

But this will not affect our foregoing argument. We may find that we know little about mind, but we know less about matter ; we may find that we cannot think of mind in isolation, but we cannot begin to think of matter at all except by starting from what is best known to us, that is, mind.

§ 3. People sometimes speak as if by substi-tuting the conception of force for the conception of matter they escaped the difficulties of materialism, and yet avoided committing themselves to any so-called "anthropomorphic" belief in a personal God.   The theory too seems to receive a kind of confirmation from the change of scientific thought which has substituted the conception of

D

motion for the conception of atoms or fluids. Electricity, for instance, used to be spoken of as a "fluid," and an atom was thought of as if it were a small hard piece of stuff. Other scientific hypotheses have in their time conveyed to popular language the idea of electricity rather as *motion* and of an atom as a vortex, and it has seemed to the unscientific mind as if all existence was being resolved into "force" and "motion." But it is impossible to conceive of motion without something that moves, and "force" implies the action of something on something else, just as "right" legally speaking is the claim of somebody or something on some other thing or person. "Force" can no more float about detached from anything than "rights" can exist without anybody to whom they belong or anything on which they have a claim. Speaking metaphorically we can say that "rights" constitute a society, but we are tacitly assuming that there are beings in the society who have the rights. The "rights" quite by themselves without any persons or things would not go far to build up the social state.

Just so we may say, speaking elliptically, that the universe is constituted by "forces"; but "force" is really an abstract conception which could not be conceived as existing apart from the things or spirits of the universe. The apparent ethereality of the idea of force consists in its abstractness.

Thus Matthew Arnold's attempt to express a

notion of Deity which should be less definite than
personality, as "a stream of tendency"—"a
power, not ourselves, that makes for righteousness," was full of contradiction ; the idea seemed
vast because it was vague.   A power which is not
the power of something is no more conceivable
than the roundness which is not the quality of a
round thing : it is a mere abstraction from something real.   Righteousness does not exist except
for a moral being ; there is no righteousness in
colour, nor in earthquakes, nor in science, nor in
history—except as conceived from a moral point
of view ; and only a moral thinking being can
conceive of anything from a moral point of view.

This theory, as we have said, was an attempt
to escape from the supposed anthropomorphism
of attributing personality to the Power which rules
the world, but it is necessary, if we would think of
God at all, that we should think of Him by means
of some conception, even if we think of divinity
as transcending that conception.   Every finite
form must be incapable of furnishing us with an
adequate conception of the infinite ; our endeavour
can only be to conceive of the greatest that is
possible to us, and still to remember that it is
necessarily inadequate.

Now, though we shall probably find that our
own personality cannot be thought of as self-
dependent, yet personality is the highest category
we know ; higher than matter, which is an irrational conception without the presupposition of

mind; more real than "force," which is a mere abstraction from the idea of matter or the idea of mind.

Having then set aside the initial difficulty of materialism, we must proceed to consider the scientific difficulties of religious thought, and specially of Christian thought. In the study of these scientific difficulties we must remember that science is dealing with matter and mind in abstraction; considering, that is, not their fundamental relation to one another, but only their observed uniformities of causation. We shall not therefore be concerned in the next chapters with the fundamental questions of the possibility of religion, but with apparent contradictions between scientific truths and religion so far as it is manifested in the region of external fact and history.

PART II
CRITICAL

A. THE DIFFICULTIES OF SCIENCE

CHAPTER I

DEFINITION OF SCIENTIFIC DIFFICULTIES

§ 1. LET us then consider first what are the chief scientific difficulties in the way of the religious belief of ordinary people. It would seem simple to reply that the chief difficulty is " the miraculous element in religion "; but " the miraculous element" is a very vague expression, and in its wider meaning of "the interference of God in the affairs of the world" the difficulty is double-edged ; for it is a difficulty both that God should interfere in the affairs of the world and also that He should not do so.

The root of this difficulty is that the scientific explanation of the universe seems to be all-sufficient ; therefore the difficulty, as we have said, is double-edged. If the scientific explanation of the universe is adequate to account for all the facts, it would seem that there is no need and no room for the action of a Divine Personality. If, on the other hand, we believe in God because we see signs of

His action in the world distinct from the natural course of events, it would appear that such action must abrogate the laws which God Himself has made. Thus while science shows more and more clearly that the world is subject to law, the less the world appears to need for its explanation a personal governor or ruler; and therefore any religion which, like Christianity, appears to rest historically on certain great "interferences with the course of nature" becomes more of an offence to the scientific spirit.

We must notice that in the last few years one difficulty seems to have vanished. The idea that evolution is incompatible with religion is dying out. It has become evident that if man developed from a jelly-fish, the difference between a man and a jelly-fish does not therefore disappear; and if the world has developed from a nebula, its need of a creator is not thereby diminished; for if a ready-made world demands an originating cause, a nebula, which had enfolded within it all the mysterious possibilities of development, demands no less an originator. A stone Galatea who could develop into a living Galatea does not need a lesser but a greater sculptor.

The average man has in fact got rid of the idea that "evolution" *explains* anything; for evolution is only a method of development, and can neither explain that which develops nor that which is developed. If we saw every step of the process by which a chemical compound became a living being, it would still be plainly an inadequate description of that conscious being's suffering or sin to speak of it as a common but unfortunate kind of chemical compound.   Thus "development" or "evolution" is no explanation of existence.[1]

But belief in God does not depend on the fact that science cannot yet show perfect continuity of development.   If spontaneous generation were proved, if life could have had a physical origin in the universe, if there were no gaps between the inorganic and the organic, religion would not therefore have received its death-blow. The existence of such gaps, which fuller scientific knowledge might at any moment fill up, could be no basis for religion, and a belief which held that the *only* instance of the action of God was the introduction of life into a world which had developed itself from a nebula would have no standing ground at all.

On the other hand, even though the idea of evolution is not exactly a logical difficulty, the acceptance of it often creates a kind of uneasiness in the mind.   That God should have set things going is, after all, not enough for us ; for religion then would seem to narrow itself to the acceptance of some past event, whereas any

---

[1] The very existence of such a thing as an " explanation " is not possible until the conscious creature has reached a rather high stage of development.

active religious feeling depends on the belief in a
more immediate relation with the Divine.   The
more the province of science spreads from things
physical to things psychical, the more we recognise
the reign of law in things of the soul as well as of
the body, the less the religious consciousness is
satisfied to think of God as the maker of a machine
which once set going needs no more the touch of
the maker's hand.

In opposition to this view of the relation of
nature to God is that which Tennyson perhaps
more than any other writer has commended to
the popular mind, namely, that the law of God is
every moment the act of God :

For if He thunder by law the thunder is yet His voice.

Yet even this conception of the laws of nature as
divine does not satisfy the religious consciousness if the idea of a Central Force is substituted
for the idea of a Personal God.   Personality is
the greatest and most real conception of which
we have experience ; but the scientific view of
the world seems to drive back not only our idea
of God, but even our idea of ourselves, into the
realm of force.   We tend to think of God under
the form of force, and even of our own personalities as in the last resort the product of the forces
of nature.

There is an old German legend of a lad im-
prisoned in a cell whose walls day by day closed
in upon him.   He had learned a spell, the magic

of which he would not trust, until the moment
when his prison threatened to become his grave ;
then he clapped his hands and cried upon the
unseen power for aid, and the walls dissolved.
So we sit trembling in spirit, allowing the material
forces of the universe to threaten us, to close in
upon us, but hardly committing ourselves to the
venture of trust in the unseen.

The threat is but a nightmare, for it is the
philosophy of materialism presenting itself again in
the form of science.   Let us re-state the problem
in this form.   The scientific man may say " I
do not concern myself with origins or ends.   It
may be that as matter is unintelligible except by
presupposition of the mental element, we cannot
except by presupposing a Divine mind even think
of the chain of physical causes which during long
epochs of development brought mind into existence in this physical sphere and began our
problems and our questionings.   We may be
ready to admit that there is a purpose in creation,
and an end to which all development tends.   But
these questions of origins and ends are outside
science, which concerns and can concern itself
only with the chain of causes and effects.   But
within the two ends of the chain the continuity
must be complete, for science is impossible unless
we believe it to be universal.   If it is satisfying
to the religious consciousness to believe in God
only as the Alpha and Omega—a dim uncomprehended beginning in the past with a dim

uncomprehended purpose in the future—science has no quarrel with religion : only such a religion will satisfy nobody."

§ 2. But is the argument that if law covers the field Divine Personality is thereby excluded, a sound argument?

It must be noticed that the question is now not so much of argument as of aspect. Of the two contrasted views which we are considering, the religious aspect does not shut out the universality of law, nor the scientific exclude the existence of God. But the scientific aspect of the world would seem to remove God so far off as to be unsatisfying to the religious consciousness.

Now the way in which we view facts depends, above all, on that aspect of them on which we fix our attention ; and an analogy will serve us here better than an argument.

Let us take two illustrations which must of necessity be more or less fanciful, since we cannot expect to find in any part of nature a complete analogy to the relation between the parts and the whole. Let us consider the relation between a human body and one of those living cells which devour disease germs.

Considered from the plane of the phagocyte, the body appears as an ordered system in which the whole being of the phagocyte is comprehended ; and quantitatively the phagocyte is only an infinitesimal part of the whole, dependent on the ill or well-being of the whole. There are sudden disturbances of the system, new energies, enthusiasms which set the heart beating and strengthen the healthy cells ; or shocks of fear and depression which weaken them, and give the advantage to the germs of disease. Each individual phagocyte is affected for good or ill by these stimuli, and in its own warfare the phago-cyte is on the side of some vital power of the whole system, and opposed to the forces of dis-integration. The body is a well-ordered republic where the good of each member is the good of the whole.

But qualitatively the individual, the phagocyte, is the apex of the system, for each phagocyte is a complete being in itself ; while (considered from the plane of the phagocyte) the body is no more than the totality of these and other cells. Its unity is a systematic, not a vital unity.

Thus a theory could be formed from this point of view in which the body was but a system of individual phagocytes.[1] This theory would not be concerned with any fundamental explanation of the whole corporal system, with the origin of the disturbances which affect it, nor with the question of whether there is a unity of life in the whole ; and so far as it went it would be a complete and consistent theory.

But if we turn to the human being's explanation

[1] Like Dr. McTaggart's Absolute.

of the phagocyte and of himself, we find it does not contradict but includes all that we have arrived at from the point of view of the phagocyte. For all this ordered corporal system is not less an ordered corporal system if, as we know to be the case, a unity of life animates the whole.

Let us take another example. We introduce a completely deaf man into a party of people who are watching a pianist play on a grand piano of which the lid is lifted. The deaf man watches the changing expression of musician and audience, learns that there is a sympathetic experience and understands the applause; but for explanation has only the moving fingers, the little leaping notes and vibrating wires and wood. By dint of observation he forms a complete theory, founded on sight and touch, knows what will affect pathetically, cheerfully, enthusiastically. His theory is quite complete ; he only omits one thing, the end and origin of the whole, that for which the piano was made and that which the jumping notes produce—namely, the music. His explanation is quite complete and quite correct— only it is quite meaningless. It opposes the true theory by its negations and omissions, while the real explanation of the scene does not oppose but includes all that the deaf man has discovered.

Thus the scientific view puts itself in opposition to the religious only by its dogmatic denials, not by its assertion that *this*, but by its assertion

that *no more than this*, is the meaning of the
universe.   In the religious or the philosophic
view there is no negation of the scientific conclusions, but a change of the aspect under which
we view them — a different focussing of the
attention.   Any question about the origin, the
purpose and the meaning of the whole drives us
back to the question as to whether there is not a
divine mind animating the universe and touching
it at every point; and such a theory would be in
no sense a contradiction of the scientific explanation of the universe; though it is not in itself a
scientific theory of the universe, it does not
dispense with the necessity of a scientific theory,
and we must have reasons, other than science can
give us, for holding it.

But if origin and end seem to any mind to be
supremely important, that mind must necessarily
go beyond the merely scientific conception; and
in following this philosophic enquiry, especially
in studying the facts of human or personal action,
we shall see that the scientific and philosophic
points of view are not wholly distinct, for purpose
or end is continually also cause, or even absolutely origin, and thus purpose or end enters into
the chain of causation if causation is conceived in
any complete way.

Let us return to our image of the piano and
make our scientific observer not physically but only
musically deaf.   To him the piano is the starting-
point, the vibration the intermediate link, and

music the mere result; whereas from the musician's point of view music, which is the purpose, is also the cause of the piano. The unsubstantial thing which perishes from the physical sphere as soon as it is born, is the cause not only of the material instrument which produces it, but of the special arrangement of notes on which it depends. Nay, to the deaf Beethoven the physical sound is the unessential, but the music is the eternal and fundamental.

A. THE DIFFICULTIES OF SCIENCE
—*Continued*

CHAPTER II

SCIENCE AND MIRACLES

§ 1. But although the idea of a Divine Personality immanent in the universe is thus not inconsistent with the scientific view, we have still to consider the other side of the suggested difficulty, and to ask whether special divine manifestations, such as miracles or answers to prayer, are inconsistent with the scientific and indeed with the true religious conception of the universe.   It is said, for instance, that the belief in the efficacy of prayer would involve the assumption that God can and will at man's request change the course of nature, and that the belief that God should thus "abrogate" the laws [1] which He has made is an offence not only to the scientific but to the religious spirit.

---

[1] This objection seems to gain point through a confused idea of the meaning of law ; but it has often been pointed out that the " laws " which are said to " govern " phenomena are merely the general expression of the way in which phenomena are observed to take place.

This objection however overlooks the action of personality in the world. In the larger sense, of course, human personality is as much a fact of nature as the law of gravity or electrical force ; but when we speak, as we do here, of nature as distinct from man, we must not leave out of sight the fact that man is continually changing the course of nature and suspending its laws.

Man changes the course of nature in one sphere when he arrests the spread of crime in society, when he preserves the weak who are ready to perish. He interferes with the course of nature in another region when he cures a disease, arrests an infection, when he teaches a parrot to speak and a bear to dance, or when he dams a river. It is true that in all the actions by which man suspends the course and alters the laws of nature he acts by the law of nature. He is working through social and spiritual law when he arrests the law of criminal degeneration ; through medical laws when he arrests disease ; through laws of animal imitation when he makes the bird utter human speech. It is a law of nature which he puts in operation when he changes the course of rivers. But does a belief in prayer demand that the course of nature should be altered in any other way than this ? Is there any theory of prayer which makes it necessary that God should answer our prayer otherwise than through action of the laws of nature ? If we believe in a Divine Personality at all why should we impose on the action of such a personality limitations which in no wise apply to human personality ?   Do we demand that God should answer our prayers not only for spiritual power but for peace, for fruitful seasons, otherwise than by setting in motion, as we ourselves do in our effort after these things, spiritual forces, social forces, and the powers of the earth ?

Now the laws by which the course of nature can be altered may either be known to us or unknown.   There is a tendency among the uneducated to regard any particularly striking or inexplicable phenomenon as specially the result of Divine agency — a "visitation of God," an "interposition of Providence"; and this same tendency is shown in the fact that if a prayer is fulfilled through the operation of some law which is well known to us, or if the progress of science shows that some event reckoned as a miracle can be, as we say, rationalistically explained, our first impulse is to exclaim that such things are not the action of a Divine Personality at all—the desired event no more an answer to prayer, the apparent miracle no longer an act of God.   Let us take two instances.   Without branching into a discussion of historical evidence, let us take for granted the theory of the Exodus given by M. Naville in his account of the excavation of Pithom.   It may be thus briefly summed.   The Red Sea probably extended much farther north than at present : the shallow " sea of weeds " can to this day be driven

back by a strong wind : the Israelites were told to
encamp between the Migdol or "watch-tower" and
the sea ; and the evident reason for a " Migdol "
at this place is that the sea was liable to be driven
back, which would allow the incursions of Arabian
tribes.   Israel then turned back from the caravan
road, sought this less certain outlet, and gained
on foot the passage at the seasonable opportunity;
while the chariots of their pursuers, hindered by
the returning water and wet sand, were unable to
overtake them.   The first natural impulse is to
say that we have no reason to think it was God
who delivered the people, if the deliverance
was worked through successful generalship taking
advantage, in almost superhuman difficulties, of a
quite providential combination of circumstances.
With our " almost superhuman " and " quite providential " we gently put away from ourselves the
possibility of some special Divine action.

Or again let us take the case of a patient at the
point of death, given over by the doctor, who yet, as
he is bound to do, applies the extremest remedies.
The patient prays, and as he prays, contrary to
all expectation he revives, and believes the prayer
is answered.   Then with returning health the
following considerations present themselves : the
medical remedies were applied, and effort, determination, hope, gave force to a failing heart.
Therefore the recovery, however unusual, was
natural.

Was it therefore not an answer to prayer ?   As

the scientific difficulty disappears, the reason for believing in the efficacy of prayer seems to vanish also.

But unless we are determined that religion and science must necessarily be opposed, there is no reason that we should cease to believe that these events were the result of divine action because they were brought about by means of the laws of nature. Certainly if we believed in God *simply* because a break in the chain of natural causation demands some divine action, our faith would be disturbed. But if our belief is founded upon any wider basis than this it is still unshaken.

§ 2. But again divine interpretations or answers to prayer might conceivably take place by means of natural laws of which we are still ignorant. It is evident that in the present state of our knowledge there may well be at work laws and causes which are unknown to us, for even many of the laws by which we ourselves effect our purposes are incompletely known. It may be said without paradox that the greatest revelation made by the progress of knowledge is the vastness of the unknown : when we stretch our imagination to picture empty space beyond space, the scientist knows that empty space is fuller than we can conceive ; we begin to realise how tiny is the compass of the sounds we can hear or the lights we can see in the ocean of waves of sound and light : deep calls to deep and atom calls to atom across all deeps. It is only unimaginative ignorance which can ever make us suppose that we know a millionth part of the laws and causes that can be known.

But the unknown is, in the process of science, continually becoming the known. Thus the scientific objection against miracles cannot be simply that they are the results of unknown laws or causes. This would be an impossible objection, for a law must be unknown before it is known, and instances of an unknown law must be observed before the law can be understood. We have experienced in our own time for instance, a great revolution of the scientific attitude with regard to one whole class of phenomena which have been called miraculous—the miracles of healing; for science has of late made many new discoveries with regard to the mental element in bodily health and illness, and the effect of suggestion on the physical functions. Instances of healing, once apparently isolated, have thus been connected with a large mass of observations concerning self-control, hypnotism and the action of the unconscious mind, and thus the miracles of healing in the Gospels present comparatively little difficulty from the scientific point of view. For the progress of science shows that the facts which appeared isolated were not really beyond its province ; just as the spring tide touching dry bunches of seaweed on the shore shows that they are not, as they seemed, beyond the reach of the sea.

§ 3. But again it may be said that the main
objection of science to miracles is not that the
law of their occurrence is unknown, but that
they appear to be in contradiction to known
laws.

Now apparent contradiction, as we have pointed
out, is often the opportunity for new discovery in
science ; and it even may be said that the absence
of apparent contradiction is due to our want of
perception, since our knowledge of laws and causes
is so small compared to their total sum.   We
ought to see far more clearly than we do the
ragged edges and incompleteness of scientific
knowledge.   Röntgen rays did not begin to exist
at the time they were discovered ; they were
always exercising effects which we either did not
notice or ascribed to a wrong cause.

But again we see throughout nature that the
laws of a lower region are truly in a sense contra-
dicted by the action of causes of a higher order.
No arithmetical law contradicts any other arithmetical law, but directly we emerge out of the
region of abstraction every one and one becomes
something more than two.   When each one and
one is a *thing* having qualities and powers, each
acts upon the other, and the two in any kind of
conjunction have qualities which each singly did
not possess.   Even a pair of identical ornaments
in decoration possess a quality artistically which
is absent from each singly.   A pair of magnets
together exercise an influence which each separ-

ately does not possess, and from a pair of complementary living creatures the whole world is
overspread.   Yet the laws of number are preserved unaltered; though the one thing and
one thing are more than merely two, their arithmetical quality is unchanged.   And in another
region the inorganic particles which gravitate
downwards are lifted by plant life upwards;
for life at once suspends and fulfils the laws
of the inorganic world, and—life itself is the
miracle.[1]

Finally, when we come to the region of
conscious spirit we find that man, as we have
said, is continually altering the course of nature
and suspending its laws.   Yet the continuity of
nature is not thereby broken, for the only way in
which man can alter the course of nature is
through the laws of nature.

§ 4. But there is one thing in the course of
events of which science cannot take cognisance,
one thing which is distinctive of personal action
—that is purpose.   If we can see purpose in the
direction of our own life and the lives of others,
purpose worked out through difficulty and opportunities, sorrow and joy; if we are constrained to
confess

> With mercy and with judgment
> My web of time He wove;

if we see in the same way a divine purpose in the

---

[1] Cf. Hegel's *Philosophy of Religion*, vol. iii. p. 119.

course of history — here is something which is quite out of the province of science. Belief in a Divine Providence guiding the natural course of events is quite unaffected by scientific difficulties or scientific explanation.

A. THE DIFFICULTIES OF SCIENCE
—*Continued*

CHAPTER III

SCIENCE AND MIRACLES

§ 1. IF the foregoing conclusions are correct, if the whole process of science is to reduce the unknown to the known and to discover new truth under apparent contradictions, why is there any special difficulty in the case of the "miraculous" unknown, and what does the "opposition" between religion and science really imply?

There is an ambiguity in this phrase which confuses the issue. The "opposition" between religion and science may mean either the opposition of science (*a*) to certain religious *ideas*, certain conceptions of the miraculous; or (*b*) opposition to certain alleged *events,* that is, to the actual occurrence of certain facts said to be miraculous.

(*a*) Now, as we have seen, there are some fundamental religious principles to which science cannot be "opposed" because it does not come in contact with them; such as the belief in Divine Providence working through natural law, known or unknown.   On the other hand, there are certain conceptions of the miraculous to which science is essentially opposed.

(b) But when we speak of the " opposition " of science to certain events said to have occurred, we may mean simply that science can put no seal upon the facts, because there is no sufficient evidence for them; or we may mean that the events are necessarily or usually regarded under some conception which is essentially opposed to science.   In the former case the events are on the same ground as any other asserted event which cannot be scientifically substantiated, but in the latter case there is a real opposition.

We have then these two classes of so-called opposition.   First, the merely unsubstantiated event; here there is no real opposition but merely a lack of support.   Secondly, the real opposition to certain general conceptions or to certain events in so far as they are regarded under such conceptions.   Thus the real opposition is an opposition of ideas, and between acceptance and opposition there lies a large region of asserted facts, religious or otherwise, which science can neither support nor reject.

§ 2. There are two main conceptions of the miraculous which are in radical opposition to scientific conceptions.

In the first place science always demands a continuity of causation—the existence of some means by which a result is accomplished; and in the history of Christianity we come across certain miracles which seem to allow no possible continuity, to leave no place for instrumentality. The miracle of the feeding of the five thousand is a miracle of this kind.

We shall touch later on the question of the historical evidence for the miracle, but certainly the scientific difficulty is not *only* that the miracle has never otherwise occurred nor that the laws by which it could be brought about are unknown, but the root of the difficulty is that even the imagination fails to find any possible continuity of causation, any intermediate links whatever between the blessing and breaking of the bread and its increase; nor can we even feel that the substances so produced could be identical with those produced by the ordinary familiar processes.

But is this difficulty more inherent in this event than in other miraculous or even natural events? The continuity of causation is an established scientific principle, but it is never actually present in the series of events as observed, or even as imagined by us. There are always gaps in the continuity of causation as we know it; but as the zoetrope whirling before one's eyes makes us see not a succession of postures but one moving figure, so our minds, moving quickly and familiarly from point to point, do not see the breaks but view the process as continuous.   The child who, puzzled by the mystery of birth and ingeniously connecting observations, suggested that lumps grow in the fields and calves come out of them, was in fact believing in Milton's miracle "the grassy clods now calved"; but no less really, older people who know certain signposts on the road of birth and ignore the stretches of road between, are believing in a miracle.   Each point as they know it does not and could not produce the next, without the intermediate link which they know not. No one knows all. Thus the actual series of events believed in would be miraculous, if gaps in the known chain of causation can make it so. But in the case of natural events, although certain links only are known the chain is conceived as continuous, each stage of production as we know it is a link in the chain, only it is not capable of producing what we seem to see it produce.   In the popular notion of the miracle on the other hand, the chain is not continuous, and the miracle is supposed to consist in the fact that the result is effected without any natural means.

But it must be remembered that this is only the popular conception of a miracle, and that there is no particular reason for regarding popular conceptions in religion as more authoritative than in science or any other subject.   If then we admit the possibility of unknown laws at work, by which through a continuous chain of causation the effect is produced, the general conception of the miracle in this respect will not be unscientific, although no scientific acceptance of the miracle is possible unless the unknown laws on which it depends are discovered.

§ 3. Secondly, the whole conception of science is opposed to the idea of an event which is not an instance of some general law, and therefore to any idea of miracle as a single arbitrary event.

But here we must draw an important distinction between a unique event and an arbitrary event. An arbitrary event is really an uncaused event, but an event may be unique because it depends on conditions which have only once been realised and can never be realised again. For instance, if there is such a thing as spontaneous generation it was to all intents and purposes a unique event; for even if at one period there was an outburst of spontaneous life, it is so far out of cognisance that it must be thought of as a unique group. The whole condition of the world at the present moment is a unique event, it can never again be realised. But it is in conception universal—under exactly the same conditions it would be realised again. Let us apply this idea to the great miracle which is at once the central point and the greatest difficulty of Christianity—the resurrection of Christ. In so far as the resurrection of Christ is regarded as in essence a universal event, in so far as Christ is regarded as "the first begotten from the dead," it is not opposed to the scientific conception. On the other hand, the resurrection of Christ was undoubtedly preached as a unique event, the conditions of which can never again be realised.[1]

Since this miracle then, although necessarily conceived as unique, is not necessarily conceived either as arbitrary or uncaused, it is not fundamentally opposed to the whole conception of science. Yet scientific acceptance can only be based on sufficient evidence for it as a fact; and in considering the evidence for the occurrence as a fact we must necessarily connect it with the class of cases to which it lies nearest, namely, with that power of mind over matter which seems to be manifested in the miracles of healing.

§ 4. But the scientific view of miracles brings us to the border-land of science and philosophy, to the edge of a gap which nothing has and nothing can bridge, where spirit turns to survey its correlative and contrast—matter—its mysterious partner and opponent. The relation of mind and matter is a mystery which no science can touch and no philosophy explain; though the point of contact is perfectly familiar to us, namely, the connection between the physical brain and the immaterial thought of the conscious being.

[1] It does not seem to be suggested in the New Testament that the resurrection of the Christian will be in all respects similar to the resurrection of Christ, but that for the greater part of mankind the natural body must first " see corruption," and that those that are alive " will be changed " without the experience of death ; whereas it is said that Jesus saw death yet " saw no corruption."

Science shows how material changes in the brain accompany each thought; but though dogmatic materialism may assert that such material changes *cause* the thought, this is a mere assertion; and philosophy on the contrary demonstrates that the material brain itself is an irrational conception, an unmeaning term apart from the hypothesis of a thinking mind.

But mysterious as the nature of this connection is and always must be, it is a familiar and fundamental fact that an immaterial idea has its first intimate connection with a material brain, and through material instruments causes changes in the material world.

Wherever consciousness exists there is a point of contact between the material and the immaterial world.

I am placed, let us say, opposite a gate by which my dog is standing. I can only move the gate by setting in motion a train of material circumstances,[1] beginning with the movement of my arm. But if I wish to move that other material thing, the dog, or the dog's tail, I have the choice of two ways: either by exerting material force of the same kind that I use to open the gate, or more easily and pleasantly by communicating (of course by means of material sound or movement) an idea to the dog's consciousness. I say, "Come

[1] It is not proved of course that this is the only way, for the possibility of the *kinetic energy*, popularly called "animal magnetism," is still an open question; but the existence and nature of any more immediate power is unproved and unknown.

here," or "Good dog," and he moves himself or his own tail.

Thus the immaterial idea, radiating from the centres of consciousness, communicated from centre to centre, works material changes through a continuous train of material causation.

But now if the scientific conception of the world is not "opposed" to this undeniable fact, it is not against the scientific conception that the divine idea should likewise produce material changes.

The entrance of the divine idea into the world, its origin, is outside science; but the mode of its working need not be so, though, as we have seen, it must produce effects which are in some sense "contradictory" to the effects of the lower laws of nature: changes in "the course of nature" must ensue.

§ 5. But it may be said science cannot admit of the sudden entrance of a new divine idea into the world. The divine idea is "disembodied," and this renders the case different from the case of human ideas which have material antecedents, or at least material accompaniments, and of which the brain is the material instrument and point of connection with the material world. What similar point of contact could there be between the divine idea and the material world?

It has been suggested that the human mind may be the direct channel between the Divine

F

Personality and the material world. Why should the divine idea be limited to this channel if matter cannot be even rationally thought of apart from mind? If the human mind has the body in which it is enshrined as its point of direct contact with the material world, we must, if we believe in the Divine Mind at all, suppose it to be in contact with every point of the material world. We cannot conceive a divine idea making a new entry upon the scene of the world as an isolated event; divine ideas must be for ever entering if the Divine Mind is continually touching the material universe at every point.

CHAPTER IV

SCIENCE AND PERSONALITY

§ 1. But if the Divine Reason is, as we have supposed, the personal cause of natural law, how can it be also the cause of exceptional occurrences?

The point of view of science is here quite other than that of philosophy or religion. The universality of law is a fundamental assumption of science; and the progress of knowledge has brought more and more of the world of nature under the realm of law, showing that what appeared arbitrary is really ordered. In other words, when this scientific assumption has been extended from province to province of phenomena, the facts have corresponded to it; and if we would have a scientific view of the universe as a whole, we must assume that all existence will at last be shown to be an ordered system.

This is the infinite goal of science; it is infinitely distant indeed, but its reality must be assumed or science could not advance one step towards it. But if all existence is thus brought under the reign of law, how can science take any account of the free action of personality whether divine or human?

There seems to be, even in the sphere of thought, no room for such free action, for psychology discovers uniformities or laws even with regard to thoughts, impulses, desires and actions which seem individual and spontaneous; and we distinguish antecedent and consequent which we call cause and effect, in the mental as in the material world.

But yet we must notice one striking difference between causation in the moral and in the material world.

In any summary of the mental antecedents of an act, said according to the determinist theory to be *necessitated*, there is present in normal cases one invariable antecedent, the consciousness of a power to choose. The determinist may say that this is a mere delusion, but under circumstances varying in all kinds of ways it is the only mental antecedent which cannot be eliminated from actions which we call voluntary (viz. the only actions which we consider fully rational).

When this "delusion" vanishes we unhesitatingly class the case as abnormal, and regard the person either as having lost something essential to the rational human being, as in cases of insanity, alcoholism, and so forth ; or as being under what we call *abnormal influence* as in cases of hypnotism or of great emotional excitement personal or religious.   In such a case the agent describes his experience by saying, " I felt I was being driven" ; or " I could not help it, I had no power to choose."   But these abnormal cases of experience are also the abnormal cases of science, while psychology deals mainly with the normal human being who is acting under a sense of freedom, and whose actions yet show him to be under the reign of law.

Now, as we have already said, the reign of law is a scientific assumption, not a scientific discovery ; it is "proved" in so far as facts correspond to the assumption ; and in the material world they do in the end always so correspond.

But the assertion that science has thus *proved* that free-will does not exist contains in it a double error.   It overlooks, in the first place, the fact that here, as elsewhere, uniformity is *assumed* ; if we did not abstract the element of free-will for the purpose of studying psychological law, the science of psychology could not exist.

But, secondly, it overlooks the fact that in this assumption we are setting on one side an invariable antecedent of rational action—namely, the consciousness of the power of choice.   We are quite right in making this abstraction if we remember that it is an abstraction, exactly as Euclid is right in abstracting from " breadth " and considering a line as "length" only. But if we imagine that therefore Euclid had "proved" that "length" existed without "breadth," we should make much the same mistake as if we concluded that psychology had "proved" that man existed without free-will. If we treated the mathematical abstraction, true as it is, as a reality, we should land ourselves in an absurdity. If we treat the psychological abstraction as complete, we find ourselves with an impossible, irrational man as our subject.

The assumption that free-will does not exist seems necessary to the determinist in order to bring his knowledge in the psychological region into harmony with his knowledge in other spheres; but the assumption that free-will does exist seems necessary, on the other hand, in order to bring our experience into harmony with itself.

It is possible indeed that we are all labouring under a delusion, but if so it is a delusion unlike all other delusions. In ordinary cases the existence of a permanent delusion is the sign of an unsound mind. Here the absence of the "delusion" proves the mind to be unsound. This is not in itself conclusive : Galileo seemed a madman in a sane world, whereas he was a sane man in a deluded world. Even so the determinist may be right, although even he himself labours continually under the delusion which he rejects, for if he is a normal man he feels and acts as if he had the power of choice.

If then he allows his determinism to be a bar to his acceptance of religion, he must rationally relinquish every other judgment which assumes free-will and responsibility. He must not in his heart attribute blame even to the Government if he happens to be in the Opposition, nor to the Bishops if he belongs to the Free Churches ; the Sultan of Turkey must have no moral guilt nor Gordon any merit ; the one is but an anti-social type and the other a desirable specimen. Of course he may encourage the delusion of free-will in others, since the feeling of responsibility is a motive to desirable social action ; but he will clearly recognise that he does not even *choose* to do this, he has been "determined to do it." The most scientific determinist will break down in trying to accommodate language and thought to his theory, and the subtle differences in attitude and action to which the theory would constantly lead are quite unsummable ; it only does not lead to them because determinists are usually neither very subtle nor very consistent. In fact no perfect determinist ever existed or can exist.

But some determinist might urge that the sense of freedom, the consciousness of a power of choice, merely arises from the fact that man is able to determine his *actions*, that the will can choose one or other course of conduct ; but that the determination of the will itself, the motives under which it acts, are not in a man's own power.

Now this argument seems to rest on the creation of a new entity ; it seems to set beside the man himself, his motives, his action, another existence—*his will.* Where is the warrant for this new entity ? The will is the man, as the mind is the man. If we would distinguish the quality in him which we call will, it is power of choice whether of action or of thought or affection. In all these he is (in a normal condition) conscious of a certain measure of freedom, greatest perhaps in action, less in thought and less still in affection ; he is conscious both of a direct and indirect power of determination, conscious that he can stimulate affection by thought, conscious that he can control thought by action. When a man confesses to inability to control affections, thought or action, we know that he is in some degree in an abnormal condition.

Now the admission of any freedom at all neutralises the determinist's position. Yet any theory which does not take account of the consciousness of freedom is untrue to the facts of experience.

The clue to the difficulty is that the conception of law in the external world cannot be extended in exactly the same form to the world of human thought and action without banishing as a delusion one main characteristic of all normal human experience, the consciousness of choice. This characteristic, too, does not rest merely on invariable observation, but the principle of freedom

is a principle which we cannot possibly dispense
with in rational life ; it is so important that even
those who do not believe in it would seldom wish
to eradicate the idea, for fear that all social and
rational life would go to pieces ; morality and all
high religions appear to rest upon it. Such a
consideration indicates that the fundamental mistake lies in the attempt to extend exactly that
conception of law which is drawn from the physical world to the rational world. To do this
is indeed to put the cart before the horse, for
our only direct experience of causation, it must
be remembered, is in our own volition, that is
in the heart of the "delusion" itself. It is from
our own power of determining actions that we
first learn what causation means, and look for it
in the external world.

But to admit free-will is not to banish law :
there is a conception of law which the most
fervent believer in free-will must accept ; he
recognises it in his experience and finds it
present in his practical action. All rational practical action rests on the assumption that there are
laws of character and thought combined with an
originating and self-controlling power. We find
this involved in our dealings with animals and
men ; we know that certain inducements and threats
will produce certain effects ; but at the same time
we allow for choice, and strengthen as far as we
are able the sense of this power. We have not
got into true connection even with an intelligent

dog while we are directing his actions by simple impulses of fear or greed, and we cannot gain this relation until we can make him feel that his own action can merit approval or disapproval ; in the same manner the rational relation with a child is arrived at, when the child realises that it is possible to be either in a condition of opposition or correspondence to a much stronger power, and that voluntary submission is the thing required of him. All our action in dealing with children or with any number of individuals is based on a double principle of law and freedom. We "board out" workhouse children in the country because we expect the conditions to act on them in certain ways ; we are prepared for varying degrees of success, not only because of the variations of the circumstances and tendencies of the children, but because we expect their wills to act within these opportunities in varying ways. If all our dealings with others depend on the recognition of these two principles, the very conception of acting upon others at all rests upon an assumption of the same originating element in ourselves.

But when we cannot eliminate an element of our experience which is at the same time the basis of a necessary principle of practical action, it would be no more logical to reject it because it does not harmonise with our other general conceptions than it would be to reject any phenomenon which stood the test of experiment, because it did not appear to be an instance of any known law.

§ 2. Finally, then, it is necessary for us to ask how far the rational mind must be affected by scientific acceptance or rejection.

It is so obvious that no rational mind can comfortably accept a theory of positive knowledge and yet be unaffected by its conclusions, that we do not need to emphasise this side of the matter; on the contrary, we must guard against giving too much weight to scientific acceptance.

In the first place, as we have seen, science can neither accept nor reject such beliefs as lie outside its province; as for example the belief in Divine Providence. Again, science cannot accept facts on insufficient evidence or theories yet unproved; yet we may have reasons which warrant us in believing that these events did occur and that these theories are true. Further, in a very familiar instance, we are compelled to believe in an experience which is in actual conflict with fundamental scientific assumption—namely, the existence of free-will, which is essential to rational action.

Thus, though we cannot limit rational belief to belief scientifically provable or proved, reason will lead us, where scientific evidence is wanting, to seek for evidence in other regions of thought; and further, to discern if there should be any vital necessity for believing things which science must positively reject.

When we believe, without seeking further reason, that which science cannot accept ; when we believe, without essential necessity, that which science rejects, we cannot be said to hold a rational attitude of belief. Our belief may be courageous, it may be heroic, it may even turn out to be correct, but it is not rational.

Nevertheless, even in a case when our belief on some specific point is not rational, yet it is possible our general attitude may be rational. We must consider how far it is rational to expect to hold an independent position of acceptance in every item of our belief. The "Grammarian" may rightly spend moribund years in appraising the value of the "enclitic δε," but he cannot in the course of his life examine such details in more than one subject. Yet a human being is bound to have beliefs on many subjects if he is to live at all, more if he is to live rationally. To cast away all ideas which he has not assimilated, and all authoritative utterance which he has not tested, may be as well the sign of an intellect below the average as of an intellect above it.

Thus we are led back to the questions proposed at the outset which will have to be dealt with in their order. For the moment however we must address ourselves to the first question of the direct or historic evidence for Christian beliefs, including some which cannot at present be accepted from the simply scientific standpoint.

B. THE UNCERTAINTIES OF HISTORY

CHAPTER V

THE RECORDS OF CHRISTIANITY

ROUGHLY speaking, historical evidence is of two kinds, the evidence of records and the evidence of results ; the records of the life of Christ are not the only historical evidence of evangelic and apostolic times ; the historical evidence includes the results, the whole influence of Christianity in the world, especially its results in the Christian Church and Christian life.

It is evident that the historical criticism of results must be on somewhat different lines from the historical criticism of records ; but the two are not quite independent, for records are among the first results. St. Paul did not set out to write a record of Christ, but his gospel, which is the earliest record, is the result of his activities among the churches. On the other hand, all "results" up to the present time must be given us through records.

It is to the records that we must first address
ourselves to find an answer to our questions, and
no difficulties, real or fancied, can justify us in
setting them aside ; for here we have a body of
writings for the existence, the character and the
influence of which we must somehow account.
The rejection from the scientific point of view
of the miracles recorded would not by any means
disburden us of all difficulty, for the record of
the miracles is there ; and as it cannot be
"uncaused," we have somehow to explain, if not
the miracle itself, its record, and in some cases
the results of its acceptance.   How did it come
to be recorded and to be believed?   Are the
results such as could be due to mere belief in an
event, or are they consequences of its reality ?

For the answer we have again to go to the
science of history.

If we cannot accept the miracle as a fact, we
may rationalise it and explain it as a natural event
coloured and exaggerated by the imagination ; or
we may class it with other miraculous tales whose
laws and developments the science of folklore is
trying to discover.

But any such explanation of a scientific difficulty must itself be scientific.   Even pure invention has its laws and its limits, and a fanciful or
inadequate explanation is sometimes less respect-
able than an uncritical acceptance.

Whether or no an explanation is adequate
depends greatly on the sum of historical evidence

and the amount of historical weight laid upon the incident. In the case of the miracle of the money in the fish's mouth, there is comparatively little historic testimony and very little depends historically on the incident; perhaps also this story may be paralleled with other traditions more or less similar.

But the miraculous feeding of the five thousand, on the other hand, has the full weight of all the evangelic testimony; the incident, miraculous or otherwise, was a critical point in the human history of Christ's life, and a rationalisation of the incident which would attribute the miraculous colouring to the ordinary tendency of tradition to exaggerate, has to reckon with the possibility that one or more of these accounts is the narrative of an eye-witness. On the other hand, if the rationalisation were such as to leave untouched the Messianic import of the event and its relation to the discourses which follow, it is conceivable that the scientific difficulty of the miracle might be met without raising a new historical difficulty as to the fact of its record.[1]

[1] The discourse which follows the incident is a turning-point in St. John's Gospel: it was then the people saw the "sign" and prepared to make Jesus a King. Now, if by "signs" (vi. 14, σημεῖα or σημεῖον ; vi. 26, σημεῖα) ; and "sign" (vi. 30, σημεῖον ; A.V. quite unnecessarily translated "miracle" in the two first places, "sign" in the third) is meant merely the *miraculous* feeding, the discourse loses its significance and even its coherence. It is difficult to understand how those who would make Jesus a King because of the *miracle*, whom He could reprove because they thought more of the food than the *miracles*, could say immediately after, "What sign then—or miracle—showest thou, that we may see and believe in thee?" But if the "sign" means the Messianic character of the feeding (cf. Lightfoot, *Biblical Essays*, The Authenticity

For the results of historical criticism show beyond question that we are not dealing with simple
fabrication, but with more or less reliable historical
testimony.   Much of this testimony is not
seriously assailed by scientific criticism ; for the
question whether there is sufficient evidence for
belief in the main outlines of the life, death, and
teaching of Jesus Christ, is not really the same
question as whether there is enough evidence for
the birth narrative, the miracles, or the resurrection.   The human record is closely, or even
essentially, connected with the miraculous record,
but the question of the authenticity of the two is
not simply identical.[1]

As regards the evidence for the life of Jesus
Christ, certain main facts are practically un-
questioned : the approximate dates and the main
circumstances of His life and death, the main
tendencies of His teaching and the opposition to
it ; the personality of some of His disciples and

and Genuineness of St. John's Gospel, i. p. 24 ; cf. Sanday, *The
Life of Christ in Recent Research*, p. 104), it is comprehensible that
they should, in the first enthusiasm, intend to proclaim Him as Messianic
King, and then on the reproof try to elicit whether He Himself would
give the sign of the feeding as a proof of Messianic claims.   The ignorance
of the multitude that an overwhelming "miracle" had been performed
would not, of course, in itself prove anything, for it might not have been
observed by any but the disciples ; but the "sign" was patent and the
rationalisation of the miracle (see the suggested explanation of the
parallel passage, Mark vi. 30-44, Menzies, *The Earliest Gospel*) would
not diminish the significance of the whole incident as given in the Fourth
Gospel.

[1] I do not mean here to give any opinion as to whether the evidence
for the supernatural incidents is *as strong as* that for the natural events ;
but merely to point out that the question of evidence in the two cases is
not *the same*.   Identical evidence to a probable and an improbable event
is not of identical value.

their belief in His claims and in His resurrection—
all these facts, with some details about His
betrayal and the sacramental meal in which He
participated the night before He died, would not
be questioned by any serious critic.

Where then do the chief difficulties arise
from the historical side?

There is first the apparent probability, stated
with more or less plausibility or crudity according to the education and intellect of the man who
feels it, that where so many details are in doubt,
the main outlines of the life, character, and teaching are in doubt also. In its crudest form the
difficulty was presented by a countrywoman who
complained that her summer lodgers told her the
Bible had been so much revised that not a word
of it remained the same. Yet even analogy
should show us that the difficulty is entirely a
matter of proportion. An accurate sketch, even
an accurate photograph, is not infallible as to any
one of its details, yet the main outlines are not
therefore untrustworthy. One figure wrong in
the beginning of a long arithmetical calculation
will have its error multiplied throughout. But
the general view of a life and character where one
inaccurate detail corrects another is quite different
from such a chain of deductive evidence. A
biography may give a true and living picture of a
man, and yet the verification of its details may be
very incomplete.

In the hands of the vulgar opponent of

Christianity, and of some opponents who need not and should not be vulgar, this difficulty is used to show the great uncertainty of Christian teaching. The disingenuousness of the attack is transparent, for such opponents speak with unconcealed contempt of the conflicting voices of divided churches, and at the same time treat this babel of tongues as the only utterance of Christian truth.

The second difficulty is perhaps more serious. Though the main outlines of the life, character, and teaching of Christ are established, active Christianity cannot be content with main outlines ; it must ask whether there is sufficient historical evidence to prove the fundamental doctrine of Christ's person and the truth of His teaching. The strength of the attack on such beliefs lies in the fact that two lines of argument appear to converge on one point : on the one side it is urged that there is not enough historical evidence to prove the truth of fundamental Christian belief; and on the other, that the comparative study of religion shows that such beliefs are but one stage of natural intellectual development, and that the survival and spread of Christianity among the most civilised nations is accounted for by the fact that it was the religion, on the whole, best fitted for man's needs, and most suited to promote his progress.   After enquiring into the material of the historical evidence for Christianity, we shall therefore have to consider how the natural development of religious ideas bears on the question.

Let it be noticed that we are not yet addressing ourselves to the question whether there is sufficient *evidence* for more than the main outlines, still less whether there is *a reason for believing* more than the main outlines. We cannot too often insist on the fact that, in questioning the historical evidence or the scientific evidence for the Christian belief, we are only questioning one kind of evidence ; and that, besides the possibility of there being evidence in other regions of knowledge, it is sometimes true that we have reason for believing that which we have not sufficient evidence to prove.

B. THE UNCERTAINTIES OF HISTORY—*Continued*

CHAPTER VI

SCIENTIFIC ACCURACY AND ARTISTIC TRUTH

§ 1. WE often find that our difficulties in certain matters are not due to the subject itself so much as to the expectation with which we approach it. The difficulty of drawing a house in perspective for instance is not due to the fact that the lines appear to converge, but to the fact that we cannot overcome our expectation that lines which are parallel will also appear parallel. Our very knowledge that they are parallel prevents us seeing that they do not look parallel.

Just so, if we survey all the records of the past through the medium of our own ideas of historical accuracy, we may often create for ourselves difficulties not inherent in the subject.

We could not in any case expect to find records of an early time written, as they would be written now, from an evidential point of view. The idea of historical writing was different: a

writer aimed at conveying a body of teaching
and presenting a personality ; to carry this into
effect he might compose speeches as freely as we
assign motives ;[1] but such a presentation, if it
is infinitely more powerful than, let us say a
scientifically accurate record, is not in the same
way evidentially strong.   But though discrepancies
between different narratives of the same event
show the want of scientific accuracy, the way in
which they affect the value of historical evidence
is a subtle question ; for there is no doubt that a
certain amount of difference between the narratives
of different authors confirms their authenticity.

Let us take a very simple illustration of this
principle.   Let us suppose ourselves entering a
room where easels with drawings are grouped
round a centre.   We pass from easel to easel,
finding on each board the drawing of a face, and
the likeness between them proves that they are
all representations of the same face.

Yet in one sense the drawings are all unlike,
for a tracing of one would not agree in any single
line with any of the others ; and this very fact
is evidence that all are drawings of a real solid
thing—drawings from different angles of a real
face, not of a portrait.   If we found two quite
alike we should know that one was a copy of the
other, and thus from the point of view of evidence, a forgery.

[1] Cf. Schürer, *History of the Jewish People in the Time of Christ*,
vol. i. p. 98.

There is another point of unlikeness. The style and treatment of each is different; yet if we found one style throughout we should be forced to conclude either that all the drawings were by the same hand, or that one master had so far impressed himself on many minds as to make the drawings reflections of his own idea rather than of the impression made by the model.

On a desk behind the circle of easels we find an impression from a copper-plate etching. In one sense it is more unlike any of the portraits than they are unlike each other; for colour, material, handling, all are quite different. In another sense, outline for outline, proportion for proportion, the face is exactly like one of the portraits, *i.e.* it is a representation at second-hand of the model. Yet much has had to be changed : brushwork has to be expressed by line, colour interpreted in terms of black and white.

But there is a curious difference between it and the portrait of which it is a copy. The face corresponds to one of the portraits on an easel, but that portrait gives the head only, and the black and white artist has drawn the figure. We begin to look along the circle of the easels, and we are arrested by the next drawing, which gives the outline of a figure almost exactly like the etching; but the lines have been slightly changed to adjust the angle of the head to the figure, and this has given a slightly different expression, a more vigorous or eager pose. The black and

white artist thus has been the editor of facts seen
through two pairs of artists' eyes; his own bias
too is probably not wanting.

We leave the drawing-school and enter a
science class-room, where we pass from desk to
desk, noting in different writings the record of
the same experiment. The records are not
identical, but when they differ we do not say
"This student saw the facts from a different point
of view"; but "This student made a mistake
here and lost a point there."

Now it is evident that our critical standard
differs according as we are aiming at artistic
truth or scientific accuracy. The two are not of
course quite different—a portrait which is *really
quite accurate* must be also absolutely like.
Either artistic truth or scientific accuracy carried
out to perfection involves the other; but a portrait may be very accurate without being very
like, or very like without being wholly accurate.
The point of the difference really is that when we
speak of scientific accuracy we regard truth as
being, so to speak, on one plane, all measured
by one standard; when we speak of artistic
truth we distinguish between the fundamental or
essential, and the superficial or the detail; we
recognise that any artistic rendering of truth
must be partial, and therefore we regard that
as true which is essentially true to some characteristic, even if it expresses but one side
of truth, and even if it is in some degree

inaccurate.   Hence the differing aspects may both be true.

Now the author of an historical record or a personal record may be as essentially an artist as the portrait painter.   The region under consideration is great and varied, including not only outward acts and circumstances, but tendencies, impulses, thoughts; so that we cannot expect, as in a scientific record, to include *all* the material of a certain kind.   A choice must be made in history or biography as in landscape or portrait painting, and the choice must depend as much on the author as on the painter.   Nevertheless, it is not arbitrary : if Turner accentuates blue and rose tones and Constable paints with blacker shadows, they may both be right, though both undoubtedly neglect something; but if a portrait painter chose to ignore, let us say, the noses of his subjects, he could not possibly be right.   The nose is an essential feature in the artistic rendering of a face.

On the other hand, it is quite possible that a historian or biographer may be more akin to a simple observer than to an artist, and it is clear that in history as in biography the scientific view has of late gained ground on the artistic view ; it is by no means so certain that such proportions more truly present a personality or pourtray the spiritual forces of a time.   If ancient historians had too elastic a view of the facts of the past, we are not therefore necessarily right in

giving the proportion we do to the facts, compared to the spirit of the age in which they took
place ; and in personal records the modern biographer sometimes tends to give the mere
materials for biography, while the reader is left
to form his own view of the literary taste of a
man from a list of his favourite authors, or of his
humour from a string of his jokes.

Without doubt the spirit and essential character of acts and persons is what we seek in
historical or personal records, and though these
may be disguised by inaccuracy, they may also
be buried under detail.

To seek behind the inaccuracies of a record
its essential spirit and truth, there is requisite
not only a discerning and accurate mind, but a
sympathetic and perceptive temper ; and a presentation which is not evidentially strong may be
inherently convincing.

We may prove by dates and diaries that a
certain picture is Romney's portrait of himself,
but when we see the picture it brings with it an
inherent conviction.   Here the man leant back
with his palette in his hand and looked with his
own artist's eyes into his artist's soul.

§ 2. In studying the records of the life of
Christ then we must keep our minds open to
recognise that discrepancy may be, not only a
proof of inaccuracy but one test of authenticity ;
that we must allow for the different aspects under

which the writers would view their subject according to their characters, and according to their relation to the person they pourtray; and that their portraiture, if not evidentially conclusive, may be inherently convincing.

Again it is evident that writers are affected by the beliefs of their time, which will colour their accounts of certain incidents. The actuality of demoniac possession which seems to us to require the strongest proofs, would be as much taken for granted by writers of that race and age as telegraphic communication by ourselves. That prodigies of discovery and invention should follow the steps of science seems necessary and natural to us; that miracles should accompany the steps of a divine teacher seemed equally necessary and natural to them. They will not give evidence to convince us, but the existence of what we should consider adequate evidence for such beliefs would be, from the historical point of view, itself a miracle of anachronism; and to demand such a record would therefore be unscientific. The very fact that these beliefs were natural will show us that they need not affect the simple trustworthiness of the writers in other matters; and our only scientific attitude will be to consider first what our material *is*, instead of making up our minds what we should wish it to be, independently of the conditions of the time.

The difficulty nevertheless remains a very serious one, for many of the incidents to which varying or discrepant testimony is given are incidents that include the miraculous element; there are only two stories of the nativity, and they differ in character, aspect, and circumstance; there are several accounts of resurrection appearances and some of them are difficult to harmonise. The only miracle which has unanimous and obviously harmonious testimony is just that which the scientific mind finds almost impossibly hard to accept — the feeding of the five thousand. Thus where the weightiest events seem to need clearest and most uniform evidence, we get varying testimony; or where the scientific difficulty is greatest and the spiritual import is least— where we most easily might relinquish an incident—a fourfold harmonious voice proclaims it true.

But another difficulty presents itself : we find in all the records a strong idealising tendency, corresponding in some degree to the distance in time from the events recorded.

If then, allowing for this tendency, we read history backwards and transport ourselves in imagination past even the earliest records, down the diminishing scale to the moment of the events recorded, we might ask whether we have more here than the sketch of a powerful personality, wise, lovable, divinely-minded above the average—a man whose strong and sweet influence and tragic end left an undying devotion among His followers and a lasting mark on history.

But we must here note briefly what we shall develop later, that idealisation is not always the result of an inventive faculty, but of an imaginative perception which can penetrate to the root of things.

Again it is often urged as a difficulty that the writers, whoever they may have been, were not unbiassed : their nation and religion had given them certain expectations ; the influence plainly exercised over them had made them believe their expectations were fulfilled. Before they began to record they had become partisans.

But this difficulty is created greatly by our own prepossessions : the demand for "unprejudiced witnesses" is entirely inappropriate to the nature of the case. Whatever theological doctrine we may hold, it will hardly be disputed that the influence of Jesus Christ is the strongest personal influence in recorded history ; yet the external circumstances of His life are particularly obscure, there is nothing for history to take hold of.

The short public preaching from one to three years, in an obscure province of the Roman Empire, of a young artisan, a man who died as a common criminal, no Judas or Theudas even, but one apparently unable to effect so much as an ordinary Judaic revolution, still less to inaugurate a Maccabæan independence — what is there in this to induce any one to describe it who had not experienced a potent secret influence ? As soon as the influence had begun to spread, though mainly through the lower classes of the Roman Empire, it begins to be noticed by secular writers, as in the letters of Pliny or the allusion of Suetonius.

The demand for an unprejudiced witness is strangely unhistorical. It is the demand for one who has the perspicuity to see the weighty bearing of obscure facts without the sympathetic or imaginative nature which would be influenced by them. One part of the evidence for Christianity on the contrary, is that the writers *are* "prejudiced." It is because of the inherent conviction of the story recorded that the witnesses cannot be unprejudiced.

Yet when we combine these various difficulties they seem to throw considerable doubt on the validity of the records. And when we search for external reasons for believing in the records, our search reveals that the authorship is not provable on external grounds alone ; that the earliest was written some time after the events recorded, when memory had had time to grow less distinct ; and that, though often discrepant, the records are yet not independent.

We cannot in the present argument urge the plea of revelation in support of the truth and authenticity of the records, for we should have first to show reason for believing that the records are "revealed." On the other hand, since we are dealing with the records as simple human documents, we must expect the writers to be affected by the beliefs of their time ; the very fact of their writing proves them to be "prejudiced" witnesses, that is, witnesses deeply impressed by the greatness of the personality they are describing ; and this fact of their deep impression would naturally result in a developing perception, they would necessarily be unable to understand such a character at once. In fact our rational attitude will be, not to ask whether the testimony of these writers altogether conforms to the canons of our time, but to the ideas of their own ; not altogether whether their evidence is adequate, but whether it is appropriate.

We cannot possibly in so brief a treatise try to weigh the proofs of historical evidence. All we can do is to attempt to determine on a rational attitude, in view of the fact that on the one side these difficulties exist, and that careful and expert study is necessary even to fully appreciate them ; and on the other, that the mass of testimony with which they deal cannot be set aside and that the truth of it is vital to us.

B. THE UNCERTAINTIES OF HISTORY—*Continued*

CHAPTER VII

EVIDENCE FROM RECORDS

§ 1. LET us then briefly describe the material of our evidence, considering in connection with it the conclusions of sober Biblical criticism on the subject of the date and authorship professed or implied of the records. In concentrating attention on professed authorship we do not overlook the importance of traditions about authorship, but the establishment of a tradition has not the same bearing on the genuineness of the writers. The Epistle to the Hebrews was at one time traditionally ascribed to St. Paul ; because it is clearly not written by St. Paul, it is not therefore a forgery, since the author makes no such profession. On the other hand, if it could be proved that the Epistle to the Galatians was not written by St. Paul, it would be pseudonymous. Now, although pseudonymous writings cannot be coarsely classed with forgery, they belong to imaginative rather than historical literature; many touches must be thrown in to produce verisimilitude, and it is difficult to distinguish these from the historical foundation on which the whole may be constructed. If the Epistle to the Galatians were pseudonymous, although it might give an essentially true picture of the historical situation, it would not give us any assurance that St. Paul's picture of his conversion was necessarily genuine. A pseudonymous writer must almost necessarily give imaginary *foreground* touches even on a historical background. Thus a pseudonymous writer, like a writer of historical fiction, may write in good faith, but his work is not genuine in the same sense as an historical work.

In judging the substantial truth of the records so given, we must not merely consider the good faith of the writers nor their intention to be accurate, but we must bear in mind that the conditions of the time, the beliefs, expectations and "bias" of the writers must, humanly speaking, affect their records; finally, in summarising our results, it must be remembered that testimony which is not adequate to bear the sole weight of proof may yet be perfectly suitable to its time and adequate to its own share of proof. It is an everyday occurrence that we believe, and rightly believe, assertions about people and events not because the evidence is overwhelmingly strong, but because it is suitable to what we previously knew and believed.[1]

We trust a statement because we know that such and such a person would have acted in the way reported ; or that such and such an event might have been expected. The evidence which would not by itself bear the weight of proof is conclusive because it is suitable. Occasionally even the thinner thread of evidence is the most credible. Some one has acted with a full and secret generosity ; we hear it reported or conjectured, and the very fact that we do not hear the story on very close authority forms part of the suitability of the evidence, if the man designated is wont to do his charities in secret.

§ 2. Among the records of the life of Christ the first in point of date is the *record* given by St. Paul. We have to cull this *record* from allusions in letters which presuppose and refer

[1] At the time when the above was written (October 25, 1904), a singularly illustrative incident had just occurred. Mr. Justice Grantham, in his evidence before the commission in the Adolf Beck case, gave details of an earlier case under his jurisdiction in which a prison warder in the hospital ward was accused of the murder of a prisoner on the first-hand evidence of a fellow-prisoner, who described what he said he had seen. The previous character of the warder seemed to belie the story, but the doctor's testimony confirmed the evidence, for he declared that the injuries from which the man had died had been inflicted about five hours before his death, when the warder alone had access to him. The evidence, said Mr. Justice Grantham, was complete. He considered however that the *nature of the case* discounted this corroborative evidence. A man who had borne so good a character as the warder *could* not, he thought, have committed such an act ; and he finally charged the jury, "If you believe the evidence you must convict this man ; if you trust me you will not." The jury acquitted, and subsequent events proved the warder innocent.

H

to teaching previously given. Even destructive criticism would now allow that at any rate four epistles of St. Paul (those to the Romans, the Corinthians, and the Galatians) were of undoubted authenticity.[1]

In order not to involve ourselves with details of historical criticism, we will consider only such allusions as are found in these epistles. Here we know the writer, and that the letters were written only some twenty to thirty years after the death of Christ.[2] But we find from the epistles that, in whatever way the writer had learnt the facts of our Lord's life and precepts,[3] he took the opportunity, on a visit to Jerusalem, of carefully comparing his teaching with that of the other Apostles, and found it to be both correct and adequate.[4] Whether or no he saw Jesus Christ during His life on earth is not certain. "Though we have known Christ after the flesh," "Have I not seen Jesus our Lord?" might seem to imply this; but at any rate it was not any appearance during His earthly life, but a vision after Christ's ascension on which St. Paul laid stress, and to which his conversion was due. He professes

---

[1] There is a Dutch school of writers which denies the authenticity of even these epistles, but their view is rejected by the majority of critics in other countries.

[2] According to Harnack (*Chron.* p. 237), the conversion of St. Paul followed closely after the crucifixion. Thus his evidence must be classed as contemporary, and St. Paul may even have been in Jerusalem at the time of the crucifixion.

[3] Cf. not only Gal. i. 16, but also 18, ἀνῆλθον εἰς Ἱεροσόλυμα ἱστορῆσαι Κηφᾶν.

[4] Cf. Gal. ii. 2, 3, 6-9.

CHAP. VII EVIDENCE FROM RECORDS 99

that he received his gospel from Christ Himself and not from man; but some expressions would be consistent with the interpretation that it was the spirit, the "mystery" of the gospel which St. Paul received by revelation, while he learnt the simple historical facts as his circumstances and intercourse with others afforded opportunity. But in any case we can, from the human side, consider St. Paul as a competent, if not a first-hand witness; and though indeed we should expect that a man of such marked and original genius would see events in another light than the "dry light" of science, it still remains to be proved that "dry light" is the best light for the inspection of history or of character.

In these four epistles St. Paul states that Jesus was of the family of David; that He had twelve disciples, of whom Peter and John are mentioned; that He was betrayed at night—on the same night on which He instituted a sacramental supper; that He was crucified, died and was buried; that He rose the third day, and after His resurrection was seen of Cephas, of James, by the twelve Apostles, and then by five hundred disciples, of whom the greater part were then still living, and to whose testimony he appeals; finally, that He appeared to St. Paul himself.[1]   In addition to

---

[1] 1 Cor. xv. 3-8. It is generally assumed that this vision was seen at the time of St. Paul's conversion, and it is somewhat remarkable that St. Paul's own account of the conversion says only that he saw the *light* and heard the *voice* (Acts xxii. 6 ff., xxvi. 13 ff.), though he says distinctly that "in ecstasy" he saw Christ at Jerusalem (xxii. 17, γενέσθαι με ἐν ἐκστάσει

these facts St. Paul gives several aphoristic sayings, some of which we seem able in substance
to identify with those in the Gospels ; e.g. "they
which proclaim the gospel should live of the
gospel." [1]

There is no reason to suppose that St. Paul
was ill-informed or inaccurate ; neither, with one
great exception, would it be disputed that St.
Paul's ethical teaching is substantially Christ's
teaching. For though the universalism of the
message may be claimed as St. Paul's, that which
is morally the root of universalism, the revolt
against formalism, must be admitted to be one of
the most characteristic features of the teaching of
Christ.

§ 3. The next record in order of date is probably the second Gospel. It is generally agreed

---

καὶ ἰδεῖν αὐτόν). Yet Ananias says of Christ that He appeared to Paul
in the way (ὁ ὀφθείς σοι, ix. 17), and Paul reports Ananias as having
said that Paul himself was appointed "to see the Just One." The terms
here are very explicit (xxii. 14, γνῶναι τὸ θέλημα αὐτοῦ καὶ ἰδεῖν τὸν
δίκαιον καὶ ἀκοῦσαι φωνὴν ἐκ τοῦ στόματος αὐτοῦ). All this seems to refer
more exactly to the ecstatic appearance at Jerusalem. Again in St. Paul's
second account (xxvi. 16 ff.), Christ says : "I appeared to thee . . . and
will appear to thee" (ὤφθην σοι . . . ὧν τε ὀφθήσομαί σοι), which is
followed by a clear account of Paul's mission corresponding to that given
to him in Jerusalem. If we would reconcile all these passages it would
appear that we must not press ὤφθη to mean necessarily a manifestation
in human form (though it is the word used of all the appearances in 1 Cor.
xv. 3 ff.), nor draw so hard a line as is sometimes done between "ecstatic
vision" and so-called "objective" appearance. On the other hand, if
we insist on pressing details, "have I not seen (ἑόρακα) Jesus our Lord"
(1 Cor. ix. 1), would seem to refer to the vision at Jerusalem rather than to
an appearance in human form outside Damascus.

[1] Knowling, Witness of the Epistles, p. 320.

that it was written before A.D. 70. The author writes simply and colloquially; he makes no allusion to the birth and early life of Jesus Christ; he describes in detail Christ's ministry in Galilee as if it lasted about a year, and records more fully the events of the last week at Jerusalem. All the main facts agree with those given by St. Paul, but there are variations in detail. The words spoken at the institution of the Last Supper, for instance, are not exactly the same.

The end of the original Gospel is lost, so that we cannot be sure, apart from the affirmation that the tomb was empty, what witness the author would have given to the resurrection; but the mention of the angelic promise that Christ should be seen in Galilee makes it probable that some such account as is contained in Matt. xxviii. 16 must have followed. Many of the speeches in St. Mark's record are aphoristic like the few sayings given by St. Paul, and the identity of the main outlines of the ethical teaching would not be disputed. Jesus Christ is called "Son of Man," perhaps in the more strictly Messianic sense, and the whole book is said to be the "Gospel of Jesus Christ the Son of God."[1] The resurrection is not directly brought forward as

---

[1] Mark i. 1. "The evidence for the omission of these words" (*i.e.* υἱοῦ θεοῦ) "is weighty but meagre. Westcott and Hort (*Notes*, p. 23) relegate them to the margin as a secondary reading, but hold that 'neither reading can be safely rejected.' Possibly the heading existed almost from the first in two forms, with and without υἱοῦ θεοῦ." Swete, *Gospel according to S. Mark*, l. c.

the proof of Christ's divinity, for the belief in the divinity is established before the crucifixion; but the book is historical not philosophical, so that we should not expect much theological theory.

This Gospel is anonymous, but criticism is tending to concede the traditional authorship of John Mark,[1] whose mother had a house in Jerusalem at the time, and who accompanied St. Paul afterwards as his attendant on some journeys. The Gospel possibly embodies much that had been previously cast into form for oral teaching, though some vivid touches—the bright squares like flower-beds formed by the multitudes on the green grass [2]—seem to show the hand of the eye-witness. There is no great improbability in the theory that the author introduces himself as the "young man" in the scene in Gethsemane.

Our third Gospel is professedly a history written from sources, and about A.D. 80 would now very generally be given as the date. The writer is anxious to assure his correspondent of his competence for the task; he has not been an eye-witness indeed, but he has thoroughly acquainted himself with all the sources of information, and has been taught by those who were eye-witnesses. His main source of information is common to the first three Gospels. He has also access to information shared by St. Matthew only; and

---

[1] Tradition refers to St. Peter as the informant of Mark. Cf. Eusebius, *H.E.* iii. 39.

[2] Menzies, *The Earliest Gospel*, p. 144.

though his record is nowhere identical with that of the fourth evangelist, to some extent it covers the same ground : some personages, Martha and Mary for instance, are common to the two, and though the actual incidents related are not found in both writers, the Mary and Martha of St. Luke are characteristically the Mary and Martha of St. John. St. Luke tells briefly the running of Peter to the tomb, St. John relates it in detail and with expansion. Periods of our Lord's life indicated by St. Luke might well fit on to those elaborated by St. John.[1]

It is evident that St. Luke had, as he says, special opportunities of knowledge. It would appear, as Professor Ramsay points out, that one of his informants was a woman, for St. Luke tells us more than the other evangelists about the women among our Lord's followers. This is more especially noticeable in the account of the nativity, where the events are related as they concern the

---

[1] Exact adjustment is not easy or even possible, but compare the chapters (Luke x.-xviii.) containing the teaching of the so-called Peræan ministry with the short sojourns at Jerusalem (John x., xi.), each ending with an escape into desert places (John x. 39, 40; xi. 54). The comparison of the sequence of events is evidentially most interesting. If the fourth Gospel were proved to be an imaginative work, one would say that a great deal of its historical background had been supplied by such material in St. Luke. Yet there are corrective and supplementary touches in the handling of the material peculiar to St. Luke, as well as of that given by the other Synoptists. For example, the fourth evangelist, who alone narrates the spear-thrust, says, "He showed them His hands and His *side*," where St. Luke says, "He showed them His hands and His *feet*"; and the figures of Martha and Mary, so lightly touched by St. Luke, and by him alone of the Synoptists, are prominent in the fourth Gospel, by their connection through Lazarus, with the incident which there appears critical in leading to the death of Jesus.

Virgin Mother. Again, St. Luke appears to have a special source of knowledge about the Herodian party; and Professor Sanday[1] points out that St. Luke (and he alone) mentions twice Joanna the wife of Chuza, Herod's steward, who may thus have been his special informant on both subjects.

In this record the form of the literary man, the touches of the editor are evident. St. Luke gives (whether correctly or not) dates, names of rulers, etc.; he adds reasons and explanations where St. Mark records impressions; if we compare the two accounts of the healing of the palsied man, we find the bearers in St. Mark's account are uncovering the roof before we are aware that they have stopped pushing at the door of the court, while St. Luke explains how they went up to the top of the house. The facts are not given with untutored vividness, but assimilated, explained and related in a literary manner. The identification of the writer of the third Gospel with the editor of the Acts is obvious; but whether he were indeed the "beloved physician," the companion of St. Paul, is still in dispute, as some critics would assign the "travel document" to an author distinct from the compiler.

The first evangelist tells us nothing about himself or his sources, but his record reveals much; it brings out his Hebraic instinct, and a desire to show the fulfilment of prophecy so strong that in some cases the prophecy seems warped, and in

[1] Hastings, *Dictionary of the Bible*, vol. ii. pp. 639, 644.

others the fulfilling incident seems at first sight
exaggerated or even invented.   The record is
evidently composite, and a moderate advanced
criticism would assign the compilation to A.D.
70-100.[1]   Besides the matter which it shares with
the other Synoptists or with the third only, there
are some incidents not paralleled elsewhere, and
also a very large body of teaching (only found
fragmentarily in St. Luke) which carries inherent
conviction of authenticity.   This comprises the
sayings of Christ, which, correctly or incorrectly,
led to the identification of our first Gospel in
whole or in part with that ascribed by a very
early writer to St. Matthew.[2]   The evangelist
incorporates an account of the nativity and the
events following on it, which, while agreeing in
its main facts with that of St. Luke, is quite independently written, and is told moreover not from
the point of view of the mother but from that of
her betrothed husband.

Thus so far as we have gone, we have one
complete chain of events to which sometimes all
the writers testify, incorporating in their account
one tradition ; sometimes they all agree, and
sometimes a single voice testifies to teaching or
incidents which accord with the main scheme so
well that in the term "Synoptists" we lay stress
on the fact that all these writers view Christ's life
under one aspect.

---

[1] Harnack gives 70-75 as the probable date, with the exception of some
later additions.   [2] Papias, c. A.D. 145-160.   Eus. *H.E.* iii. 39.

The independence of the accounts and their variations in detail increase when we come to the last week of our Lord's life, and in the records of the resurrection this independence grows so much that it seems to amount to discrepancy.

§ 4. The fourth Gospel, on the word of the writer himself or on that of the disciple who attested it for him, professes to be the account of an eye - witness; it bears indeed so absolutely this character that we can only say that the writer wrote as an eye-witness whether or no he was one, yet it is as certainly evident that he wrote a considerable time after the events which he records.

How does this account compare with the others? The record covers such different ground, shows such different sides of character, and takes such different views of certain incidents, that we are again confronted with two pairs of alternatives—either the account is supplementary or it is not harmonious; either it is corrective or it is contradictory.

We cannot do more here than touch in a general way on the differences which are minutely argued in many books, and which are well known in outline. There are, it is said, differences of schematization between the apparent one year's ministry of the Synoptists and the three years' ministry in St. John's Gospel; there are chronological differences on individual points, such as

the day of crucifixion, or the time of John the
Baptist's apprehension ;[1] differences in the persons
or classes of persons mentioned,[2] and in the types
of miracles related — the healing of demoniacs
and lepers for instance, frequent in the Synoptic
Gospels, is entirely absent from the fourth ; there
are differences not only of style but of tone and
tendency in the speeches—the long discourses, the
mystical raptures, the allegories of the fourth
evangelist contrast with the aphoristic sayings
and the parables of the Synoptists ; there are
differences, according to some critics, in the char-
acteristics of our Lord, the simplicity, the human
portraiture of the Synoptists being exchanged for
a figure more mysterious, more typical ; and
differences in the development of the teaching
about His person—from the outset His Messianic
character appears.

Some critics find an anti-Judaic strain in the
writer which enhances all these differences, and
argue that the exhibition of philosophic thought
makes it impossible to believe that the writer is
one of the band of Galilean fishermen.

Other critics regard the discrepancies as corrective and the additions as supplementary, in
accordance with the tradition that St. John wrote
his Gospel for the very purpose of supplementing
previous accounts ;[3] and certain close agreements

---

[1] It is not, however, impossible to harmonise these accounts.
[2] Scribes, Sadducees, publicans are not mentioned.
[3] Eusebius, *H.E.* iii. 24.

with the Synoptists, even in the very phraseology,[1] combined with these differences seem to show that the fourth evangelist could not have been unaware of the assertions he was adding to or correcting.

Thus St. John alone relates the speeches of the one certain witness of the baptism, that is, the Baptist; and these speeches of the "Voice" as he calls himself, attesting the divine sonship of Jesus, and the spiritual outpouring which he describes as "like" the descent of a dove, correct, and in correcting explain the more materialistic description of the signs at the baptism given by St. Matthew and St. Luke.[2]   St. Luke's allusion to the preaching in the synagogues of Judæa[3] points to other ministries there than that of the last week recorded in detail by the Synoptists; and since the popular enthusiasm about the prophet of Galilee was so held in check by Jesus Himself that it did not even threaten a revolution, the determined hostility at Jerusalem and the quick dealings of the Passion week could not be accounted for without some such events as are related only in the fourth Gospel.[4]   The whole

---

[1] *E.g.* cf. John xii. 3-9; Mark xiv. 3-8; John vi. 7; Mark vi. 37.

[2] Matt. iii. 17: ἰδοὺ φωνὴ ἐκ τῶν οὐρανῶν λέγουσα.   Luke iii. 22: καταβῆναι τὸ πνεῦμα τὸ ἅγιον σωματικῷ εἴδει . . . καὶ φωνὴν . . . γενέσθαι.   Mark has a less objective statement, especially if the doubtful ἐγένετο, i. 11, is not read.

[3] See Westcott and Hort's text, Luke iv. 44.   In view of Luke's use of the name Judæa to denote the whole country, both Galilee and Judæa proper, this verse seems to refer to a ministry that was not confined to only one part of the land.

[4] Cf. also the implications in Matthew xxiii. 37 ff. : "*How often* would

account of the trial, with the accusation based on
an actual speech which St. John alone records,
becomes clear and sufficient by help of the explanations he gives.

As regards the alleged differences of style even
the more conservative critics would allow that the
fourth evangelist combined many sayings into
one discourse, indeed this construction is quite
obviously indicated in the sixth chapter;[1] but
even apart from this it is open to question
whether the style of the speeches ascribed to
Christ in the fourth Gospel is wholly unlike the
style of those recorded by the Synoptists.   The
mystical rapture[2] reported by St. Matthew and
St. Luke is in the tone and spirit supposed to be
most distinctive of the fourth evangelist, and some
aphoristic sayings, " some short sentences which
are in close or partial agreement with the
Synoptics," are found in his Gospel.[3]

But besides the difficult mystical discourses,
there is another substantial difference between
the fourth and the first three Gospels, namely,
the much greater part devoted to showing what

I have gathered thy children together ($\pi o \sigma \acute{a} \kappa \iota s \ \mathring{\eta} \theta \acute{\epsilon} \lambda \eta \sigma a$) " ; in the response
to the message about the colt at Bethany (Matt. xxi. 2, 3 ; Mark xi. 1-6 ;
Luke xix. 29-34) ; in the arrangement about the room for the Passover
(Matt. xxvi. 17 ff. ; Mark xiv. 12-15 ; Luke xxii. 7-13).

[1] Cf. John vi. 25 and 59.

[2] Matt. xi. 25-30 ; Luke x. 21, 22.

[3] Drummond (*Character and Authorship of the Fourth Gospel*, p. 17) "for
instance, v. 8, ' Arise, take up thy bed and walk,' hardly differs from
Mark ii. 9, and John xiii. 38 comes nearest to the words of Luke xxii. 34.
For a full list of such allusions and resemblances, see Westcott's *S. John*,
p. lxxxi. *seq*."

we should usually call the intimate side of the
character of Jesus Christ.   Even from the naturalistic point of view it is impossible to believe that
such a personality should not have had more,
and more intimate converse with his immediate
followers than the Synoptic writers give us,
especially in the time immediately preceding His
death.   If there had been no such intimate converse it would have implied an unexpected lack
in the emotional side of the nature ; we might
have felt perhaps something of the chill which
falls upon us, even through all the beauty of the
death-scene of Socrates, as we realise how much
the philosophic development had outrun the
human feeling.   But from the picture which the
Synoptists themselves set before us, and because
of the immense effect of the personality of Jesus
on His contemporaries, we are led to expect no
such lack ; rather from the comparison with any
full and beautiful nature which we have known,
or which biography has revealed to us, we see
that there must have been a greater inward
development than we are told.[1]

We have hints of such intimate converse in the

----

[1] Cf. Browning's address (*One Word More*) to the

                    moon of poets !
Ah, but that's the world's side, there's the wonder,
Thus they see you, praise you, think they know you !
There, in turn I stand with them and praise you—
Out of my own self, I dare to phrase it.
But the best is when I glide from out them,
Cross a step or two of dubious twilight,
Come out on the other side, the novel
Silent silver lights and darks undreamed of,
Where I hush and bless myself with silence.

Synoptic Gospels, not only of the teaching privately given to the disciples,[1] but of personal emotion as when Jesus looked on a young man and loved him,[2] or stretched his hand impulsively to a leper, then having healed him chid him sharply for penetrating uncleansed into the city.[3] The Synoptists give us, too, revelations of His personal feeling—of grief, of anger at hardness, of trouble of spirit,[4] above all, the revelation of the agonised struggle in Gethsemane to conform the human will to the divine.   But all this intimate side of character and feeling is far more developed in the fourth Gospel, and yet characteristically corresponds to the Synoptic account.   The first advance of friendship, " Come and see,"[5] so humanly different from the authoritative call "Follow me," reminds us (of course without the humour) of the homely accost, " Zacchæus, make haste and come down ; for I must stay in thy house to-day."[6]   St. Luke's account of the friendship with Martha and Mary harmonises with the picture in the fourth Gospel, though it is slightly touched compared to the depth and range of emotion given in the great scenes of the illness and death of Lazarus.

But the passages in the fourth Gospel which make the most direct appeal to human nature,

[1] Mark iv. 34, etc.

[2] Mark x. 21.

[3] Mark i. 40 ff., 43—καὶ ἐμβριμησάμενος αὐτῷ εὐθὺς ἐξέβαλεν αὐτόν. And cf. Luke v. 12 ; Mark i. 38 and 45.

[4] Mark iii. 5 ; viii. 12, etc.   [5] John i. 39.   [6] Luke xix. 5.

across all lapse of time, and apart from all distinction of education and intellect, are perhaps
the parable of the Good Shepherd and the discourse at the Last Supper. Yet we have only
to read :

> Let not your heart be troubled : ye believe in God, believe
> also in me. In my Father's house are many mansions ; [1]
> Fear not, little flock, for it is your Father's good pleasure
> to give you the kingdom. [2]
> My sheep hear my voice, and I know them, and they
> follow me : and I give unto them eternal life. . . .
> No man is able to pluck them out of my Father's hand, [3]

to see how the feeling in the fourth Gospel is
present, though less developed, in the third.

Nor does even the strange scene of the three-
fold questioning of Peter's love [4] stand quite
alone, since we must connect it with the agonised
appeal for human sympathy, unresponded to in
Gethsemane, with the first cry, " Simon, sleepest
thou," [5] with the final ironic " Sleep on now and
take your rest," [6] and with that look the Lord
turned on Peter as He heard him forswearing
even His acquaintance. [7] If there is any reality
of human relation, the reconciliation after such
scenes could not be private only, nor tacit.

The complementary correspondence of the
Gospels is even more enhanced by the fact that
when the Synoptists give the innermost side, as
in the agony in the garden, the fourth evangelist

[1] John xiv. 1-2.   [5] Mark xiv. 37.
[2] Luke xii. 32.   [6] Mark xiv. 41.
[3] John x. 27 ff.   [7] Luke xxii. 60 ff.
[4] John xxi. 15-17.

shows us "the world's side,"—the swift action that
facilitated the escape of the disciples;[1] the un-
approachable dignity[2] which succeeded, as it does
succeed, the crisis of conquered emotion.

Such points are only illustrative of others
which might be urged as explaining the difference
between the fourth Gospel and the other three.

The balance of external testimony, particularly
as affected by new discoveries, now leaves little
margin of date between the traditional and the
"advanced" view. Many even of the conservative critics would allow that lapse of time
had somewhat blurred the outlines of memory in
the fourth evangelist,[3] and also that the tradition
on which the Synoptists draw may sometimes
very naturally have interpreted symbolic representations as if these were literal descriptions of
incidents, and preserved the simpler rather than
the more mystical sayings.

§ 5. At the present time another source of
evidence for the words of Jesus Christ is emerging
in the collection of "Sayings"[4] found in Egypt,
which are thought to date between A.D. 100 and
A.D. 140 and which probably contain first-cen-
tury elements, and may reflect a "substantially

---

[1] Cf. John xviii. 4, " went forth," cf. xviii. 8 ; Mark xiv. 50.

[2] John xviii. 6.

[3] On the other hand, it must be remembered that memories of youth are
often exceedingly vivid and detailed in age.

[4] Cf. *New Sayings of Jesus*, edited by Grenfell and Hunt, 1904, pp.
25, 33.

I

authentic tradition." Now it is remarkable that these sayings show resemblances not only to the Synoptic but to the fourth Gospels. But it is still an open question whether these sayings are genuine.

Apart from the Gospels the other notices of the life of Christ throughout the New Testament are more or less allusive and indirect.

The unknown writer to the Hebrews—imbued with the spirit of St. Paul but with far higher literary gifts, writing, as would be generally agreed, before the end of the first century—alludes in his exquisite manner, at once philosophic and poetic, to the account of the agony in the garden, to the fact that Christ suffered and was crucified outside the city, to some words He used on the night of His betrayal, possibly to the rending of the veil at His death,[1] to His ascension, and he mentions as a well-known fact that Jesus was of the tribe of Judah. His interpretation and theory of the whole history is that of St. Paul more poetically expressed.

In the Acts we have another account of the ascension which, as it is by the same hand as the account in the third Gospel, is particularly interesting as showing what amount of variety and expansion is, at any rate in the opinion of the writer, compatible with accuracy.[2] We find

[1] May not this have suggested the rather obscure imagery of Heb. x. 20.
[2] If these two books had been by different authors, we should certainly have had a large class of critics saying that the writer of the Gospel " knew

in this book, too, a saying of Christ, unrecorded in the Gospels, which is in the brief and aphoristic style of the sayings in the Synoptists : " It is more blessed to give than to receive." [1]

The sayings reported in the visions which are recorded of Christ are interesting from the critical point of view, for even if we do not regard them as Christ's own words and therefore direct evidence of the way He spoke, they are indirectly evidential of the effect of His words, and show the tradition of His way of speaking. The sayings in the Acts are singularly like the sayings of the Synoptic Gospels,[2] sometimes the

---

nothing " of the cloud nor of the two men in white apparel ; and it would have been pointed out that the author of the Acts had a different conception of the relation of the disciples to their Master, since he does not say that " He blessed them," nor that "they worshipped Him."

[1] Acts xx. 35.

[2] Compare the tender warning of the repeated name and the homely, forcible image of Luke xxii. 31, " *Simon, Simon,* behold, Satan hath desired to have you *that he may sift you as wheat,*" with Acts xxvi. 14, " *Saul, Saul,* why persecutest thou me ?   It is hard for thee to *kick against the goads.*" But since this resemblance might be attributed to the common author of both books, the following passages are perhaps even more worth comparison : the order to Ananias (Acts ix. 11) with that to the disciples at Bethany (Mark xi. 1 ff.), and to the two who should prepare the Passover at Jerusalem (Mark xiv. 13 ff.) ; the same kind of action is required in all three passages.   The brief command to do an act almost impossible to one of Jewish nurture, " Rise, Peter, kill and eat " (Acts x. 13), reminds us of the equally brief order to do an act apparently impossible by nature, " Give ye them to eat " (Mark vi. 37), and underlying both commands is a deeper spiritual meaning.   " What God hath cleansed, make not thou common " (Acts x. 15) is in the Greek more strikingly paralleled even than in the English by Mark vii. 15, 18, 19, for the word for "common " or "unclean," and the word for " purify " or " cleanse " are the same in both passages. The injunction " Fear not " to Paul (Acts xviii. 9) is peculiarly characteristic of Christ as He is presented in the Synoptic Gospels (cf., *e.g.*, Matt. x. 26, 28, 31) ; and the assurance of His presence, " for I am with thee," reminds

same words are used, θαρσεῖτε, ἐγώ εἰμι,[1] "Be of good cheer : it is I," Christ said to the distressed rowers ; again, θάρσει [2] to Paul before the trial which was to determine his Roman voyage.[3]

Whatever view is taken of the authorship of the Apocalypse, it must at any rate be assigned to an early date ; and if for our present purpose we put aside the question whether the messages were direct revelations, the speeches must be considered with regard to the light they throw on the traditional style of Christ's sayings. It is interesting to notice then, that while some sayings are almost identical with sayings recorded by the Synoptists, others—for example, " I will give to him that is athirst of the fountain of the water of life freely"; " Behold, I stand at the door and knock : if any man hear my voice and open the door, I will come in to him and will sup with him and he with me "—so closely resemble sayings of

us of the last assurance to the eleven (Matt. xxviii. 20). Compare also the correspondence and complementary nature of the Lord's prophecy to His disciples (Mark xiii. 9 ff., Matt. x. 17, 18) with that to Ananias concerning Saul (Acts ix. 15), a prophecy which is more briefly repeated to Paul himself (Acts xxii. 21) ; and the same spirit breathes in the commands as to the way in which the complementary missions are to be performed in Acts xxii. 18 and Matt. x. 23. Who would not say that one master-mind had mapped out the field and laid down the method of performance ?

Thus in the speeches of Christ as reported by the Synoptists striking parallels may be found in words, in style, in imagery, in thought, in characteristic method of command, to the vision-speeches of the Acts ; and a unity of plan and method seems to lie behind the directions concerning evangelisation. Only one of these parallels could be attributed to identity of authorship.

[1] Mark vi. 50.

[2] Acts xxiii. 11.

[3] Whereas Paul's own word (Acts xxvii. 22, 25) is εὐθυμεῖν.

the fourth Gospel that one might sometimes be
uncertain in which book they occurred;[1] and the
resemblance is accentuated when a rare thought,
uttered at a critical moment by Christ, reappears
in the Apocalypse in a message delivered through
a vision—"Be of good cheer, *I have overcome* the
world,"[2] Christ says to the disciples; "He that
overcometh . . . even as *I also overcame,*"
Christ says in a vision to His servant John.[3]

[1] This point is of great importance. The contrast between the sayings
of Christ in the fourth Gospel and those recorded by the Synoptists has
been much dwelt on as an argument against the historical character of that
Gospel. Most of those who take this view would deny the identical authorship of the Gospel and Apocalypse; they have therefore to account for the
presence in both books of a type of mystical saying which they regard as
unhistorical. The entire independence of the two books is perhaps generally
surrendered, and the fourth Gospel is sometimes regarded as a kind of anti-
Apocalypse; but it would be too much to suppose that this could account
for the mystical speeches of the Apocalypse being taken up and developed
in the fourth Gospel. Moreover fresh evidence on this point is afforded
by the *New Sayings of Jesus* (see p. 113), of which some are evidently
parallel to sayings in the Synoptists, while others have the same mystical
tendency as those of the fourth Gospel. The discoverers conclude "that
the mystical and speculative element in the early records of Christ's sayings,
which found its highest and most widely accepted expression in St. John's
Gospel, may well have been much more general and less peculiarly Johan-
nine than has hitherto been taken for granted."

[2] This is the only use of the word $\nu\iota\kappa\hat{\omega}$ in the fourth Gospel, though it
is frequent in the First Epistle.

[3] John xvi. 33; Rev. iii. 21. In comparing the sayings of the Apocalypse
with those in the Gospel we must rather criticise similarity of thought and
image than lay stress on verbal differences. For since it is probable that
Christ spoke in Aramaic, the Gospels give only translations of His words;
and since the writing of the Apocalypse shows less command of literary
Greek than any of the Gospels, verbal similarity can hardly be looked for.
Thus the difference between the cry "He that hath ears to hear . . .
let him hear" (Mark iv. 9, and parallels) and the repeated "He that hath
an ear let him hear" (Apoc. ii. 7, 11, 17, 29; iii. 6, 13, 22), is of little
matter compared with the characteristic quality of the saying. "I will
confess his name before my Father and before the angels" (Apoc. iii. 5) is

For our present purpose we need not enquire
further into the other books of the New Testa-

even more striking, from the fact that it is not a direct quotation from either
Matt. x. 32 or Luke xii. 8, but combines elements from both. So, too, the
charge " Be watchful . . . if therefore thou shalt not watch, I will come
on thee as a thief, and thou shalt not know what hour I will come upon
thee " (Apoc. iii. 3) echoes the whole spirit of the parables and the charge
Matt. xxiv. 42, 43, xxv. 13; Luke xii. 39 ; Mark xiii. 33, without being a
direct quotation.   Christ's recognition of those who endure for His sake
(Apoc. ii. iii.) recalls characteristic promises of the Synoptists' record (cf.
Matt. xvi. 25, xix. 29, etc.).

The similarities to the fourth Gospel are of the same kind : the " I
know " both the perfection and the failing of those addressed in the seven
letters reminds us of Christ's claim to *know* both God and man, divine and
human, good and evil (cf. John v. 42 ; viii. 55 ; x. 14).   In the Apocalypse
Christ describes Himself as " the Living One " (i. 17) who is ready to give
the water of life (xxi. 6 ; xxii. 17) ; in the fourth Gospel He calls Himself
" The Life " (xiv. 6) who is ready to give "the living water " (John iv. 10,
14 ; vii. 37, 38), the " fountain " (πηγή) of water is assured (John iv. 14 ;
Apocalypse xxi. 6) ; and the promise is to him who thirsts and will
come (John vii. 37 ; Apoc. xxii. 17).   We find the same contrasts of
spiritual and temporal life and death in the message, " I know thou hast a
name that thou livest, and art dead " (Apoc. iii. 1), and in the great discourse (John v.) on those who have passed from death to life, those who
are dead, who are even in the graves, and yet shall live ; and the idea of
the second death and the possibility of deliverance from it (Apoc. xx. 14,
etc.; ii. 11) corresponds to the promise of eternal life in the Gospel.   The
repeated " I am coming quickly " (Apoc. iii. 11 ; xxii. 7, 12, 20), followed
the last time by the yearning cry " Even so come, Lord Jesus ! " re-echoes
to the last words which the Gospel records, " If I will that he tarry till I
come. . . ."

The forcible broken image in the promise " I will make him a pillar in
the temple of my God, and he shall come out no more " (Apoc. iii. 12)
reminds one of the images which in John x. 9, 11 follow one another so
closely, " I am the door . . ."; " I am the good shepherd."

It may be urged that such similarities are proofs of literary dependence.
Literary dependence, however, is a difficult connection to prove unless a
common source is excluded ; the " common source " in this case would be
the actual sayings of Christ, and to exclude the common source would
therefore mean to assume *a priori* that the sayings of Christ as given in the
Gospels were not actually uttered.   Unless a common source is excluded,
literary dependence must be shown by verbal exactnesses, or by coincidences numerous or systematic above the limits of chance.   The similarities

ment : such an enquiry would involve us too much
in questions of authorship.   Many facts of Christ's
life are given in St. Peter's speeches in the
Acts, but the authenticity of reported speeches
is a difficult technical question.[1]   St. Peter's
authorship of the first epistle ascribed to him
would not be universally recognised, and his
authorship of the second is very generally surrendered, while none of the other catholic epistles
gives us much new or corroborative evidence
about the life and teaching of Christ.

we have noticed are not of this kind : they are not clear quotations nor
direct allusions to incidents which could only be known by literary record ;
they are similarities of attitude, of tone, of character.

[1] At the same time the resemblances in language and in thought between
St. Peter's speeches as reported in the Acts and the First Epistle are
most striking, and tend to confirm the authenticity of both.   Cf. *The
Credibility of the Acts*, by Dr. Chase, p. 121.

B. THE UNCERTAINTIES OF HISTORY—*Continued*

CHAPTER VIII

ESTIMATION OF EVIDENCE

§ 1. THE very fact that the records we are dealing with have been regarded as divine revelations has caused them to be subjected to a much more severe standard of criticism than ordinary narratives.   Indeed it has often been popularly assumed by many of those who believe, as well as those who disbelieve in them as divinely revealed, that a single error would destroy their whole claim to be divine.

A confusion of thought is here involved, for if we apply the ordinary methods of criticism to such records at all, we are regarding them for the time as human records affected by the ordinary kinds of human error; and we beg the whole question at issue if we assume that a divine revelation cannot be given in human and imperfect form.   Let us then ask how far the divergences of the accounts are due to such principles

of human nature as we discussed in Chapter VI.,
and are therefore differences which affect the
completeness or accuracy of the record, but not
the substantial trustworthiness of the writer, nor
the whole value of his testimony. If the fourth
Gospel is, as tradition would tell us, supplementary and corrective of the Synoptists,[1] such
human errors and incompleteness must have been
early noted and naturally treated.

In judging these accounts as human records,
we shall keep our minds open to certain expectations which common sense suggests. We find,
as we should expect, considerable agreement as
to main facts ; and that many divergences seem
due in a perfectly natural way to the date of the
record and the nearness of the writer to the
events described. As in most biographies too, we
find that the divergence increases towards the
early years ; this is natural, for the child is seldom
under inspection from the beginning, and the
importance of many of the acts and sayings of
a child cannot be known till afterwards. It is
curious how often even the birthplace of cele-
brated men is not known or is diversely reported,
yet this does not throw doubt on the later records
of their life.

In the records we are considering we find
proportionately little about the early years, but
that little is singularly interesting from the
critical point of view.   It involves an event

[1] Cf. Sanday, *The Criticism of the Fourth Gospel*, p. 71.

which science finds it impossibly hard to accept,
yet it is told independently by two writers from
the only two points of view from which it could
be known—from the side of the mother, and from
the side of the man who was called the father of
Jesus. In the nature of the case the testimony
could not be full; and the complementary character of the accounts can hardly be designed,
since there is nothing to show that the first or
third evangelist was acquainted with the other's
Gospel.[1]

Further, it would be freely admitted that the
beliefs or expectations of the time, whether true
or false, must have a tendency to colour events
and sayings and to suggest interpretations. The
recognition of this fact indeed sometimes gives
rise to an exaggerated tendency to discredit
events simply because they fit the interpretations
of the time. Let us take an instance,—the rending
of the veil in the temple at the crucifixion is
sometimes discredited because the interpretation
is so apt. But insistence on this is surely
uncritical. A thing so small in itself would
doubtless have been unobserved or unrecorded
in the tumult of griefs, anxieties and despairs
if it had not had so apt an interpretation; but
to urge that this fact is a proof that the incident
must have been invented, is to push the point
too far. Who among us cannot remember some

---

[1] It is impossible of course to discuss here with any fulness the very
strong historical testimony to this event.

small circumstance singularly apt to those who look for symbolism in events, but probably unobserved by those who despise such symbolism as superstition? The parhelion which was seen in England the same day, almost the same hour as the beginning of the Boer War, was an event of this type, not very generally noticed and even now generally forgotten; but in earlier times it was considered as symbolic of the issues of war, or even as governing them.[1] In the same way, records of coincidences and reduplication of events which very frequently happen in real life, are often soon forgotten because they are too singular to be easily believed.

But the most important point to realise is that the more many-sided the personality described, the greater variation there will be in the personal touches given by independent witnesses, for each will select that side which to him is most akin; thus not only the general influences to which the writers in common are subject, but the individuality of each will affect his record. The effect of personal influence is so complicated in action and re-action that we must treat it somewhat fully.

The more marked a personality is, the more selection there must be in a record.

Any one who has had anything to do with the

---

[1] The double reflection of the sun. It was this appearance at the battle of Mortimer's Cross which made Edward IV. take "the sun in splendour" as his cognisance.

construction of a biography will know how essential is selection; for out of the whole mass of materials—incidents, events and conversations which might be recorded—only the most necessary, the most typical, the most characteristic must be chosen.

It is for this reason that the argument sometimes used by critics that a writer "knows nothing of" the events which he does not record is so supremely irritating and so essentially unconvincing. The critic who would prove that a writer knows nothing of a fact because he does not mention it, must first show that the incident if known must necessarily have been recorded—must show that the incident had an essential relation to the purpose of the writer; for even after selection has been made of typical and characteristic incidents, those only can be included which have some relation to the purpose or point of view of the writer.

Let us suppose that the subject of a biography is an ecclesiastic, and that the purpose of the writer is to show not only what is necessary for the judgment of ecclesiastical policy but for the development of personal character; his aim will be to include what is characteristic and typical of both these sides of life. But much which might have been of interest, let us say to the psychologist, must still be omitted. A biography cannot in the most inartistic hands treat every event, every trait as of equal importance ; and even a writer with no sense of purpose, no taste and no choice, would be delivered out of a chaos of material by the exigencies of ink and paper. The very methods of writers must create differences ; even without deliberate purpose one will, by habit of systematic thought or trick of memory, cast together speeches on similar topics; while another has his imagination captured by isolated sayings.

In the cases before us all the writers had a very clear purpose. What the fourth evangelist says definitely of himself is true of all, that the record was made that readers might believe that Jesus was the Son of God, and believing might have life. The standpoint of all of them was the standpoint of belief, and their purpose was practical. But the fourth Gospel exhibits the most deliberate construction, and it is partly on this score that it has been attacked. It is possible, on the other hand, that this is the very trait which most strongly pleads in its defence that it is what it professes to be.

It was obvious from the beginning that the fourth evangelist intended to cover a different field from the others, and as we have said, the earliest tradition represents the Gospel as having been written to supplement the other three.[1] We must necessarily bear this in mind in considering the question, not only because it is traditional but because it is natural.

[1] Euseb. *H.E.* vi. 14.

It is undeniable that an artist's treatment of subjects bears the impress of his own style, and that this impress of individuality does not detract from the essential truth of the whole, rather it is in virtue of this individuality that the artist gives us eyes to see : the point of view is not the pre-judging of a fact, but is an essential part of a whole fact. One may be startled in a portrait by a great painter by a certain unlikeness to the person we have known, and come gradually to realise that the painter has seen some character-istic fundamentally true and yet not obvious to the world at large ; and we should err in judg-ment if we argued that because in a portrait there was little of the personality of the painter, there must therefore be proportionately much of the personality of the subject. What is obviously true of portraiture holds good of any presentation of character, fictional or biographical.

The explanation is of course that human personality is a thing of many aspects, and is not so limited that it can be exactly reproduced ; each man is greater than can be represented by any other man, or in any one aspect of himself ; the greater the subject the less proportionately can each man represent it, and the greater is the possible discrepancy between two trustworthy accounts.

In the case of biography the possibility of dis-crepancy is still further increased by other con-siderations. The subject has lived through years in which he himself has developed, and has been in varying relations to those who write of him. He has been the comrade of one, the friend of another, the teacher of a third.

When we consider reports of conversation, the possibilities of variation are wider yet. It is exceedingly difficult even directly after a conversation, to remember more than a few sentences verbatim ; and sometimes the less educated mind will remember these best. An old servant may have by heart the words of an order ; an expression has caught the ear by its humorousness, or commanded it by its power ; little words of frequent repetition, little inversions of sayings, tricks of speech and manner are remembered ; but sometimes, the more engrossing the subject of conversation and the more intelligent the hearer, the more he has tried to understand and to pierce to the very soul of it, the less will the actual words, except certain keynotes, certain crowning words, be remembered. Added to this, the more educated the reporter, the stronger his own personality, the more he is inclined to render the speeches in his own style ; and both consciously and unconsciously the more vividly he realises the auditors, the more he adapts his style to the impression he desires to produce upon them. If the reporter has been in the relation of disciple to his subject, he will have been under a special influence. But of what nature this special influence will be, depends upon the character of the Master.   Is the Master one who simply tried to impress certain teachings on his disciples, to make them his mouthpiece, who wished like Francis, to have "dead men, not living" for his followers; or is he one who discerned their characters, who educated their thoughts, who tried to make them assimilate his teaching? All records of Christ give us but one answer. Who surnamed the Rock man and the Sons of Thunder? Who ever united in a band of disciples men more diverse?

In trying to decide then on the limits of variation in records which may still be genuine history, we have a psychological problem of immense complexity, and the solution of such a problem on historical grounds demands not only a knowledge of history, but something which academic education does not always give—a continual observation in our own experience of the effect of one human being on another.

We have not here a single limited fact or chain of facts, the account of a battle, the official acts of a government, but a unique problem of human relations.

The question is, how far are the variations accounted for by the different relations of a unique character to men whom he has directly or indirectly affected to a singular extent?

Judging from the simply human point of view, this character in all historical probability was itself many-sided, and developed under the influence of

the sublime conception of Messiahship.[1]   Added
to this we have among the reporters men of
marked individuality, in varying intimacy of
relation to the Master.   As we are considering
the problem on the human side only, there is
much that we cannot add ; we can bring into
consideration the continuance of the Master's
influence, but must not prejudge the question
whether this influence was a still *present* and more
intimate influence after death.

§ 2. Further, the records are not all made at
the same time nor recorded at first hand ; we
have therefore to consider the possible developments in the minds of the followers.   We find
notes, convincing because humanly necessary,
saying that the disciples did not at the time
understand the meaning of events or words, but
that later they perceived their significance.[2]

But it might be said that if they did not fully
understand at the time events through which they
were passing, they may have read as *facts* into
the chain of events things which they afterwards
came to believe because they seemed explana-
tory ; this is one of the natural impulses by which

---

[1] The idea of Messiahship has of course a historical development,
and various views might be current at the same time, ranging from that of
a national deliverer to the sublime conception of one annointed by God
and sent from Him to inaugurate the reign of righteousness and to rule
over the kingdom of God.

[2] Cf. John ii. 22, vi. 60, xii. 16; Mark ix. 32 ; Luke ix. 45, xviii. 34,
xxiv. 8.

K

history is rendered inaccurate, and even sometimes falsified.[1]

But there is another process liable to be confused with such inaccuracies of memory, and a
most vital distinction must be made between the
two.

That there should be a development in the
view of the significance of events in which the
recorders once took part, and of the Person who
had once seemed to be merely the teacher and
master, may prove either that the faculty of
invention increases as the events recede, or that
the faculty of imaginative perception, of insight,
grows with the development of the mind of the
reporter, when the cloud of small events, the
"petty dust" of life has blown away.

We need only appeal to the common experience of life to understand this. Have we not
known what it is to live with a friend, admiring
and loving, and yet continually kept by reserves,
harshnesses, even all the small friction of life
from complete knowledge, till by death or absence
the friend is taken from us? A false idealism
might proceed to rub out the shadows, the
apparent flaws of the portrait, and to produce a
picture of undistinguished perfection, and thus
portraiture is falsified. But there is the truer
imagination which through the maturing process of

---

[1] *E.g.*, if the writer of the fourth Gospel ultimately came to believe
in Jesus as the Messiah, the Son of God, was he not likely to have interpreted difficult sayings of the Baptist or of Jesus Himself as direct assertions
of His Messiahship?

time disperses or shrivels up the less significant
events, putting small qualities that loomed large
in the immediate foreground into their right
proportion, and revealing the true outlines of the
character, the living and essential man. This is
the individual side of what we call the verdict of
history. "Distance lends enchantment to the
view" is an evil saying if it makes us believe
that the nearer view is necessarily the truer.

In the case we are considering the religious
consciousness had received a vast impression.
All the evangelists alike testify that the minds and
hearts of the disciples were not able to comprehend
the teaching they were receiving and the events
through which they were passing. Must we
insist, contrary to all experience of human nature,
that they still remained in this condition, or may
we allow to them as to other men that, while the
lapse of years may have blurred some memories
and kept others as sharp in outline as on the day
they were made, hearts and minds and character
developed under that intense impression, and in
maturing gradually revealed the true outlines
which had been unconsciously impressed at the
beginning?

We see this process all round us; any criticism
of character which is liberal, vital, and does not
insist on the cast-iron consistency which indicates
arrested growth, shows us such instances. We
can see this very process taking place for instance in the mind of St. Paul, as in minds

and characters which come under our direct observation.

How far development is an effort of fancy or a product of the true imagination which opens to us the realities of things beneath their appearances, is not a question which can be decided on general principles; but the principle which would exclude all development as necessarily fanciful is simply untrue to the facts of human experience.

§ 3. We have then to ask whether the differences between the records of the life of Christ are such as may be accounted for by the different personalities of the writers, influencing both their purpose and deliberate selection and the aspect under which they see and present the whole; by the mental and spiritual development of the writers which would quicken their understanding, even though time blurred the memory of actual events. Moreover we have to account not only for differences but for underlying and subtle points of unity, and above all for that substantial unity of character and personality which has impressed man in every age.[1]

It is certain that no amount of historical evidence can possibly either prove or disprove the

---

[1] This impression is not, indeed, an academic conclusion, but we have no particular reason for thinking that the "academic" or critical mind is specially qualified for judgment of character; it seems on the contrary that the academic man is at a disadvantage in such judgments, from the fact that his acquaintances and his inner experience alike are apt to be of one type—a type more developed in thought than in feeling or action.

fundamental doctrine of the divinity of Jesus Christ. Even if we grant the truth of the records, we see that this fundamental doctrine was not proved to His contemporaries beyond possibility of doubt, that it could not be proved by external fact, and that Jesus expected His disciples to believe in the resurrection because they first believed in Him.

St. Paul indeed appeals to the resurrection as proof of the divinity of Christ, and to many of the disciples it was the conclusive proof ; but how does the evidence stand for us ? Differences in the accounts have been commented on in minutest detail, and details have been even captiously treated as showing untrustworthiness where complete identity might have been held to prove literary dependence. But one fact is not always noticed. There is no attempt to give direct evidence of the resurrection. It is clearly pointed out that, unlike the resuscitation of Lazarus, the resurrection of Christ was unwitnessed. What we mean by the resurrection is an inference from two different sets of facts, both of which are by themselves well attested.

(a) *The empty tomb.*—If the emptiness of the tomb was an assertion which stood by itself, no one would attempt to say that the evidence was insufficient to prove this fact only.

(b) *Appearances.*—If the appearances stood by themselves, they are not in the main difficult to believe : it would be generally agreed that there is far too much similar evidence to doubt the occurrence of such appearances, though the details would be open to question. Even so, the differences in detail lie more in the fact that we have descriptions of different events which increase the sum of evidence, than that we have different descriptions of the same event. Even the most unusual feature in these appearances, the impression of tangibleness, is not unparalleled. Moreover when differences in the Gospel accounts are commented on, it must be remembered that the earliest testimony we have to these appearances is the testimony of St. Paul, who enumerates such instances as will carry weight, and appeals to the evidence of those still living with a genuineness which none can doubt.

But the belief in the resurrection itself, that the same body which was laid in the tomb appeared with supernatural powers after death, is the inference which the disciples made, not only from the evidence of their senses at the time, but *from all* which they had previously learnt, and believed that they subsequently learnt, from Christ Himself.

But whether we shall make this same inference depends not only on their evidence, but on our relation to the whole question of Christ's personality.

Here we have a series of records written at different times by witnesses of different degrees of nearness. " None are unbiassed," the uneducated critics cry. No, for if they were unbiassed they would have had no object in writing. " Their conclusions do not necessarily follow from their facts," it is urged. But their facts do not sum up their evidence ; the influence brought to bear on them they try to convey to others, by recording the impression which was made on them, and which through slowly maturing years they gradually realised ; it is not then historical facts alone, but this development of perception which forms for us the direct historical evidence of the life and personality of Christ.

TRANSITION TO *C*

CHAPTER IX

THE GENESIS OF RELIGIOUS IDEAS

THESE considerations suggest two questions.

Even if we were to decide that the differences between the records are just what we should expect from the circumstances of the authorship, and that they do not shake our belief in their substantial truth, still we seem to have opened the door to a large amount of inaccuracy, and to have rendered uncertain any such facts as are at variance with our ordinary experience. And this is undeniable as long as we keep to the ground simply of historical evidence. But there is all the difference in the world between believing in a religion which is bound up with certain historical facts, and believing in that religion on the ground alone of the historical evidence for these facts.

Just as our astronomical knowledge helps to prove the historical assertion of a particular eclipse in a particular year, so our religious belief may help to prove the historical facts asserted.

We are often confronted with an apparently reasonable statement that we must only believe a historical fact on historical evidence, and the assertion has the same superficial persuasiveness as the cry of South Africa for the South Africans, until we ask, "Who are the South Africans?" The cogency of the previous statement likewise disappears when we ask ourselves what we mean by an historical event.

In the largest sense an historical event is any occurrence in time; but in this sense the above statement would be untrue, for it is plain that many occurrences in time can be proved by general laws, as, *e.g.*, that whenever a pyramid with equal sides was erected the angles at the base of those sides were equal.

We cannot say that an historical event implies human action, for often it means, like the destruction of Pompeii, human suffering from an event in nature, which according to the state of our knowledge may or may not be provable from general laws. Nor can we say that an historical event is an event within the domain of history, because as we discover more of the records of ancient times the domain of history is always expanding. Nor can we say that an historical event is one which has an effect on human history, because every event has a bearing more or less direct on history. Nor again will it do to say that an historical event is an event which only can be proved from records, for the whole question at issue is whether an historical event can be proved only from historical records. Thus if this supposed axiom is more than a mere tautology, it is by no means always true.

It is continually necessary in weighing the evidence for an historical event, to fall back upon our general knowledge of laws which directly or indirectly bear upon the event, and confirm or weaken the testimony.

We say to a reporter, "you have not got the story right, or you have not got the whole story, because So-and-so *could* not have acted in the way described." Just so we may say, "records seem to point to such an effect of such an event, and we may believe it because this is the effect that would naturally follow from such a type of national character." Or again, "such a book must be of the date supposed, for its contents accord with the thought and knowledge of the time."

If then historical criticism includes, as it must, some reference to laws of character and thought or laws of the natural world, if records cannot be interpreted nor the evidence for them weighed without consideration of their scientific or psychological import, it is not possible that the historical records of a religion should be judged in any complete way without consideration of spiritual law, or without reference to their religious import. In the wider sense all cogent testimony to historical events is historical evidence.

What is called in the narrower sense historical evidence only provides us with a part of the evidence needed for our whole case. Historical evidence in the narrower sense is not enough to prove miracles, but neither is it enough to prove any fundamental Christian position; it is not enough to prove the value of the ethical teaching, for such proof requires moral judgment, and although proof is needed to show that the ethical teaching ascribed to Jesus Christ is His own, the value of this ethical teaching is itself part of the reason for assigning it to this unique figure in human history.

What we want to ask with regard to historical records, when we regard them as contributing to the proof of fundamental Christian doctrine, is not altogether "are they adequate?" but rather "are they suitable?"—not "do they amount to demonstrative proof?" but "do they go as far as any such proof can go?"

But again the ordinarily intelligent person very probably would ask whether he himself had any equipment at all for making such judgments. He has not of course a full equipment, but neither has any historical critic, nor can he have. The whole historical judgment implies, as we have seen, not only intellectual but psychological and ethical, even spiritual judgments; and the critic whose historical equipment is great is not therefore proportionately advanced in the knowledge of character. For knowledge of character, as we

prove again and again from daily life, not only
a subtle but a sympathetic judgment is necessary,
and as the subtlest portraiture without the sympathetic element is in danger of becoming carica-
ture, so the subtlest critical judgment without
sympathetic imagination becomes barren.[1]

Moreover we cannot wholly suspend judgment
because we are not experts in historical criticism.
We are not forced to be original, but we are
obliged to think, or rather, whether we think
much or little, we are forced to choose ; and continual observation of character and action, which
after all gives us the material of history in process
of formation, is forced upon the attention of all
of us who would live neighbourly at all.

Each of us too is confronted daily with the
great historic problem ; it is not only a question
of records but a question of results. The whole
of our present condition of life, so far as it depends
on Christianity or is affected by Christianity, is
the result of a huge historical structure. The
more we look upon this from the human point of
view the more stupendous does it appear. On
what foundation then is it built ? What miraculous hand has raised and still raises the edifice ?

The present is historical evidence for the past.

---

[1] Let us take an instance of a very ordinary kind. It is often argued
that the Baptist could not, as the fourth Gospel represents, have recognised
Jesus as the Son of God, because if so it would have been impossible that
he should subsequently have sent to ask, "Art thou he that should come,
or do we look for another?" Yet depression and doubt are natural effects
of imprisonment, and a mediocre writer of fiction would have imagination
enough to see this.

But here a new question fronts us : is not the religion that appears to us so unique but one of a number ? What does the present condition of Buddhism or of Mohammedanism prove ? Millions of human beings live on these beliefs : to what truths in the past do these believing lives in the present witness ? Or again if we grant that there is in the records of Christianity, in spite of apparent divergences or even inaccuracies, a mass of historical evidence for which we must somehow account, is there no way of explaining the unusual features of these records ? Is there not some explanation which will show that the doctrines of Christianity, its reputed miracles, its ideal view of a certain human personality and a certain portion of human history, are a simply natural outcome of human ideas ? If this were so we might find that the ideas esteemed divine in Christianity are simply human ideas grown somewhat larger than before, surrounded with more of poetry and better adapted to changing times and various races. If we can find some naturalistic explanation of this kind, our apology will be rendered unnecessary, for our difficulties will disappear with the uniqueness of our belief.

C. PARALLELISM OF CHRISTIANITY AND OTHER RELIGIONS

CHAPTER X

RESEMBLANCE OF DOCTRINES, RITES, NARRATIVES

The first thing that strikes us in the comparative study of religious history from the Christian point of view, is the extraordinary resemblance we find between the doctrines and rites of Christianity and of other religions, and the parallels we find between the religious myths of many races and Christian narratives. Let us take some few instances.

The outline of the story of Osiris is well known. Osiris was murdered by his brother Set—typically the evil principle—and was buried; but though dead, is still living as the righteous judge of the dead. The human soul appears at death in the Judgment Hall of the Double Truth and pleads before Osiris; the heart of the dead man is weighed in the balances, and he prays to his heart not to condemn him; the Devourer waits to destroy any condemned soul. The dead man, his body swathed like that of Osiris, becomes "an Osiris"; and his friends, performing the rites of the departed, plead for him, "Motionless, motionless are his limbs as Osiris, let them not be motionless, let them not corrupt."

The general resemblance of the outline to some elements of Christian belief is made far more striking if we compare certain definite sayings: "I am he that liveth and was dead, and, behold, I am alive for evermore, and have the keys of death and hell"; "We shall all stand before the judgment seat of Christ"; "Beloved, if our heart condemn us not, then have we confidence towards God"; "If we have been planted together in the likeness of his death, we shall be also in the likeness of his resurrection"; "We know that when he shall appear we shall be like him"; "Thou shalt not suffer thine holy one to see corruption."[1]

Again, we have alluded to the historical evidence for the miraculous nativity of Jesus Christ, but we must remember that the idea of miraculous divine birth is a common idea in many religions. The royal house of Egypt were the sons of the gods; the reliefs of Luxor temple, for instance, show that the god Amen, not the king Amenhetep, was truly the father of the king's children.

Again, we are continually reminded of the Christian sacraments by religious rites belonging

---

[1] As quoted by St. Peter, Acts ii. 27; but it is questionable if this gives the true sense of the original.

to various grades of civilisation, from barbaric, if not savage states, upwards. The mysteries of Demeter show perhaps the nearest parallel to the sacrament of communion ; for in them the worshippers sacramentally partook of the body of their deity in the form of bread. " The joint participation in this (sacrament) by all the worshippers not only renewed the bond between them and their deity, it also once more united the fellow-worshippers in a mystic bond with one another." [1]

In any such ritual we must probably trace some connection with the magical ceremonies for increasing the fertility of the land or the supply of animals for food : for man, in early stages of culture, believes that by sympathetic magic he can compel Nature to produce the effects he desires ; he acts a drama of rain-clouds and Nature sends the rain ; he scatters pieces of the beast or the corn he needs over the ground, and Nature increases the animal species and the corn springs up. To all forces of Nature and to all creatures, savage man like the child attributes personality ; and owing to this belief in universal animation, the sacrifice of beast or food comes to imply the sacrifice, not only of the material thing, but as thought advances and becomes more definite, of the materialised spirit of the thing—of the corn for example, as represented by a sheaf, by some animal, or even by a man. Thus the sacrifice of some material species, some animal hunted for

[1] Jevons, *Introduction to the History of Religion*, p. 366.

food, or some cultivated or harvested possession
is supposed to bring about an increased supply in
the year to come.

Two principles in varying form govern this
development, the idea of sacrifice and the idea of
communion. The origin of each and their combination have been variously explained. Sacrifice
has been regarded sometimes as the more fundamental idea, and believed to originate from the
desire to bring tribute to the gods. It has been
thought by some that a feast with the spirits of
the dead was the fundamental idea both of sacrifice and communion; and by others that the
custom of adoption by intermingling of shed
blood and the "totem" feast gave rise to the
ideas of communion and sacrifice; or that the
magic rites already mentioned were the origin of
all these more-developed ideas.

But whatever view may be taken, it would be
impossible in the light of present knowledge to
deny the fact that the Christian Communion is
historically connected with ideas of sacrifice and
communion which exist in very rudimentary
stages of civilisation; and that the great doctrine
of atonement has developed under the shelter of
these ideas, as they connected themselves with the
unfolding needs and instincts of the human race.
For as the sense of sin develops, the idea of its
purgation is connected with the ceremonial expulsion of the evils of the community through one
representative, and is joined with sacrifice in

L

which the guilt of the community is laid upon a
victim, as in the ceremonial of the sacrifices and
the scapegoat ; [1] participation in the victim then
becomes essential to reception of the benefits
of the sacrifice ; and the highest idea, that of
voluntary sacrifice, is necessary to the perfection
of the whole.

Here then we have instances of ancient myth
strangely parallel to what we regard as Christian
history ; of ancient ritual closely akin to Christian
ritual ; of theological ideas developed from natural
religion which are closely similar to fundamental
Christian doctrines.

What then is the connection between these
and similar elements in Christianity and in other
religions ? Are they evolved by the same process ? Are they borrowed by Christianity ? Are
they, to any great extent, borrowed from Christianity and incorporated into other religions which
have been influenced by Christianity ; as, for
instance, the apparently later addition of the resurrection of Buddha, which is thought by some to be
due to the effect of the wave of Christianity which,
in early centuries, passed over India to China. [2]

[1] The idea of the expulsion of evil—whether of demons, disease, or sin
—is common among primitive peoples.   Such customs are found among
American Indians and African tribes as well as peoples of Asia.   Dogs,
goats, cocks, and sometimes men are the usual vehicles used to bear away
the evils which it is desired to expel, and are driven with various ceremonies
from the midst of the people.   The Hebrew word translated in the Author-
ised version *Scapegoat* and in the Revised version *Azazel* probably signifies
the bad spirit to whom the sin-laden goat was driven.   For examples of
these customs cf. *The Golden Bough*, vol. iii. pp. 93-113 *et seq.*

[2] Cf. Kellog, *The Light of Asia and the Light of the World.*

On the whole, the comparative study of religion seems to show that in different parts of the world similar religious ideas, history, and rites are independently developed, because the intellectual development of man, his experiences, and his growing needs are all on similar lines; and to some extent this similarity has been increased by the influence of one religion on another.

Thus it would appear that natural religion is due to the development of the human mind; or that "man made the gods," as some in rough phrase would express it, that the ideas of deity and myths of the gods grew out of the early guesses at the origin and the forces of the world, and out of the attribution of personality to Nature and to the powers of Nature, while divine characters were conceived on the lines of human characters; and that the immaterialness of the divine beings became imaginable when man began to realise the distinction between body and spirit, while religion retained in its own service early magical rites of which the origin was forgotten. Thus, discarding grosser elements, the deities became more sublime and their worship more spiritual as science grew truer, philosophy saner, and morality purer.

In fact religion, it is urged, is one hypothesis on the way to truth. "Magic," says Dr. J. G. Frazer,[1] "is gradually superseded by religion."

[1] *The Golden Bough*, vol. iii. 2nd ed. p. 458. Cf. also vol. i. p. 63.

In magic man depends on his own strength, but finds it insufficient. Nature is stronger than he. He therefore ascribes the powers of Nature to the will, passion, or caprice of personal beings, and at this stage religion emerges; but gradually man comes to find that Nature acts according to immutable, uniform laws—thus "religion, regarded as an explanation of nature, is displaced by science."[1] If such a theory holds good of religion at all, does it not hold good of all religion? If the resemblance between religious rites, myths, and doctrines all over the world reveals to us that natural religion is the product of the general intellectual development of man, how can we believe that Christianity, when it bears so strong a resemblance to other religions, stands wholly apart from this stream of development?

Now in the first place we must make clear that the development of religion from magic is a matter of hypothesis, not of proof. It is generally admitted that Dr. Frazer, following up the theories of Mannhardt, has shown the similarity of agricultural rites all over the world and traced their origin and development; but it is not by any means generally allowed by anthropologists that the relation of such magical rites to the beginnings of religion is what he takes it to be.

Again, though many hold that the belief in a deity is developed out of a belief in ghosts, and that the idea of a spirit greater than human, an

[1] *Golden Bough*, vol. iii. p. 459.

immortal Being, is subsequent in thought to the perception of distinction between the human spirit and body, yet evidence which seems to point to the contrary conclusion is not wanting. It is quite probable that the idea of immortality does not follow but precede a recognition of the universal law of death—that it is death, not life, which has to be discovered. There is evidence to show that the belief in a creative being seems to exist among races which have not even reached the stage of ancestor worship; and there is a good deal to support the view that monotheism is not first evolved out of polytheism, but that the most primitive religion contemplates only one god, and that polytheistic myths are a later growth, in which for a time monotheism is confused and lost.

In fact, few general conclusions on the subject of the history of religion are sufficiently established to be safe as a basis of argument.

But if the evolution of religion in some way from low and alien elements is established, we have still to ask what conclusion would follow.

Innumerable differences can be shown between the doctrines of Christianity and more or less similar doctrines in other religions. It is evident that in Christianity the doctrines are far higher, purer, less material than in those religions which resemble it. But does Christianity therefore stand out of the stream of such development; and if not, does it not fall under the condemnation of being a guess on the way to truth, an outgrown hypothesis which must be sloughed off in the process of growth?

Such an enquiry divides itself into two heads.

First: If religion as a whole is evolved, is every religion thereby proved to be a mere stage in mental development?

Secondly: If so, what would be the result of this conclusion upon the question of Christianity in particular?

But before entering upon these questions, let us clear out of the way one or two points which are likely to confuse the issue; because either they are not cogent, or are in themselves excessively uncertain.

It can easily be shown by a study of the legends of saints, especially in Roman Catholic countries, that many pagan stories and customs have been associated with Christian observances: the May month of the Virgin is the month of Artemis; St. John the Baptist inherited the old pagan rites of Midsummer; old sacred wells received new dedication to saints; Christmas coincides with the keeping of the winter solstice; and Easter, it is sometimes urged, with the spring equinox.

But it must be noticed that the existence of borrowed elements does not at all affect our central question. To some extent the adoption was, no doubt, a brilliant stroke of policy on the part of priests and missionaries so to identify new objects

of reverence with old customs of reverence; to
some extent it was a result of popular eclecticism.
Anubis the guide of the dead was still painted at
the feet of Christian mummies which bore the
chalice and ears of corn on the breast; the new
began to possess the heart, while the old still
lingered round the feet.

But such transmission of borrowed elements
does not show the dependence but the strength of
a new religion. The conqueror takes into his service the ritual and the language of the conquered.
The sacred bark of the ancient Egyptians was
one of the very few symbols adopted by the
Israelites:[1] it survives to this day among the
Mohammedans, and follows its old route from
Karnak to Luxor, now as the boat of Abu
el Haggag the Mohammedan saint. This does
not prove the dependence either of Israel or
Islam on Egypt, but rather the superior force[2]
of the new religions which thus "spoiled the
Egyptians."

Let us also clear away the idea, which is
really a confusion of thought, that the developed
idea is "the same thing" as the undeveloped

[1] As the Ark. Cf. for this identification, which is not perhaps universally admitted, *The Temple of Mut in Asher*, Benson and Gourlay,
p. 125 ff.

[2] Such survivals are generally held to show the superior force of the
old religion rather than of the new, which cannot wholly destroy it. Why
should the new destroy if it can convert and use old? The destructive wars
of Israel, compared with the enslaving wars of Egypt, were a sign of the
comparative weakness of Israel as a state. But in any case the new
religion triumphs, even if it does not wholly transform what it subdues.

idea.   If the idea of duty was developed from
considerations of self-interest, the idea of duty
is not therefore the same as the idea of self-
interest, but is often opposed to it.   This is
part of the old confusion as to what is meant
by evolution.   If a man was once a baby he is
not therefore the same thing as a baby ; if he was
once a monkey, it is quite clear he is not now a
monkey.   And there is the same misunderstanding
of what growth and development mean in saying
that Christian baptism is " the same thing " as
heathen lustrations, that the Christian communion
proves " the Founder to be not superior to the
barbaric notions of the folk from whom He
sprang."   It may be truly said that the origin of
baptism cannot be explained without reference to
pagan and Jewish washings ; that the ideas underlying the communion rite cannot be historically
explained without reference to the whole history
of sacrifice through the connection of the Last
Supper with the Passover ; but it is as clear that
the Founder of Christianity gave to the idea of
communion a new and spiritual sense as that the
communicant now understands it in a spiritual
sense.   The communicant is far more likely
indeed to be entirely ignorant of the barbaric
notion than to be " not superior " to it.

Let us take a parallel case.   The history of the
development of mechanical instruments can be in
many cases very clearly traced.   Do we say that
the Maxim gun is " the same as " the matchlock,

because it has been elaborated from it ? Would it be true to say that we use the Maxim gun *because* our forefathers used the matchlock ? Our reason for using the perfected invention is because it serves our purposes ; and though we may say that we should not use the Maxim gun unless our fathers had used a matchlock, the prose truth of the matter is more clearly represented by saying that the matchlock is a step in the development or elaboration of the Maxim. Evolution can be better understood from the end than from the beginning.

Just so if religion is to be regarded as a case of evolution at all, we cannot conclude that the highest development is therefore on the level of the first beginning ; but rather we can learn from the highest form of religion the possibilities of spiritual thought, aspiration, and meaning which existed, though latent, even in the earliest barbaric notions and rites.

C. PARALLELISM OF CHRISTIANITY AND OTHER RELIGIONS—*Continued*

CHAPTER XI

EVOLUTION OF RELIGIOUS IDEAS

PEOPLE have sometimes written and spoken as if to confess a belief in the evolution of religion were equivalent to expressing disbelief in its reality. Such an idea when presented in its bare form can be seen to be illogical, for the same argument would shake the whole fabric of science. According to Dr. J. G. Frazer magic is a first attempt at scientific thought, and science is evolved by selection of the truest guesses. We are heirs to a fortune from savages; "to our predecessors we are indebted for much of what we thought most our own; their errors were not wilful extravagances . . . but simply hypotheses . . . which a fuller experience has proved to be inadequate. It is only by the successive testing of hypotheses and rejection of the false that truth is at last elicited."[1]

[1] *The Golden Bough*, vol. i. p. 449.

If this line of argument applies to science why should it not apply to religion? Why should we not consider in the same way that early religions were not "wilful extravagances" but "inadequate hypotheses," from which, by "rejection of the false, truth is at last elicited."

It is plain that the simple fact of evolution cannot prove the untruth of that which is evolved, any more than the fact of the evolution of man can prove his unreality.

If therefore the truth of a system of thought is not condemned either by the fact that it is evolved, or by the fact that the material out of which it is evolved is in part at least erroneous, the evolution of religion introduces no difficulty, unless the line of the whole evolution of thought shows that the evolution of religion is merely the elaboration of the erroneous superstitious elements of thought which have been discarded by science in the course of its development. In fact, the plea of those who urge that the development of religion proves its falsity is just this, that science rends off the garment of superstition, and religion constructs a figure out of the tattered remnants.

Now it is quite evident that the history of the development of special beliefs is still to a great extent hypothetical; and even if we were to concede the fact of some development of religious doctrine from what was at the beginning superstitious observance, it would be still unproved that science has provided all the truth of early human thought, and religion all the error.

The development of the individual mind follows similar lines to the development of the race-mind, just as the development of the embryo is on similar lines to the development of the species. The early man, like the child, no doubt applies the idea of personality without discrimination to the objects of Nature—the animals and plants, the sun and the storm; and in his first guesses about causes he attributes to all these separate powers the same kind of irrational and capricious action that he knows in himself.

It may be then that, as he finds his control over Nature imperfect and begins to realise a uniformity in Nature which will not yield to human control, he comes to ascribe to these personalities greater powers than his own. Later, there begins to emerge (if not to re-emerge) from a cloud of wild myths the idea of one power behind Nature to which is still attributed the personality that he finds is not individually possessed by the objects of Nature, while at the same time he makes truer and truer guesses at instrumental causation and the action of natural law.

If we grant that the idea of personality persists in different forms, from a first immediate ascription of personality to every animate and inanimate thing or force, up to the final belief (which perhaps has been latent from the beginning) in a transcendent personality behind all things and all forces; if we were to go further and grant that old superstitions tend to attach themselves to new forms of religious thought, and that theological ideas develop from guesses at causation, then we should have conceded the main principles that are assumed in the natural explanation of religious thought, though we must remember that this concession involves the assumption of some hypotheses at present unproved. In following this line of thought too we leave out of account for the present the evidence pointing to the conclusion that monotheism precedes polytheism; and that modern science in psychical regions is tending to re-establish scientifically certain instances of the effect of spirit, on which much primitive speculation has been built.[1]

But if these extremest guesses at the natural origin of religious ideas, rites, and legends were after all proved true, would it even then be shown that religion supersedes magic and will in its turn be superseded by science?[2]

Before the argument could prove anything of the kind two further assumptions must be made. They would be important admissions.

Firstly, we should have to assume that the idea of personality in or behind Nature is a fiction which religious thought retains and scientific thought discards.

---

[1] Notice that "we leave this out of account," *i.e.* it does not affect the argument which follows.

[2] *Golden Bough*, vol. iii. p. 458.

Secondly, we should have to assume that science and religion are dealing with the same region of experiences.

(a) But the assumption that this underlying personality is a fiction is just the central point of the argument, and cannot be prejudged at the outset. The manner in which the human mind arrives at a belief in no way proves the truth or falsity of that belief. Some anthropologists hold that the belief in personality is present in the earliest conception of the universe, and Frazer allows that "the advance of thought tends to strip the old animal and plant gods of their bestial and vegetable husk, and to leave their human attributes (which are always *the kernel of the conception*), as the final and sole residuum." [1]

Thus it is conceded that religious thought does not evolve belief in an external personality from plant and animal. From the beginning personality, as highly developed as man could conceive it from his own experience, is "the kernel of the conception."

To the scientific materialist personality is the temporary result of the forces of the universe; to the metaphysical idealist, as to all religious thinkers, even the primitive thinker, personality is "the kernel of the conception."

(b) But are science and religion dealing with the same ideas?

The savage may not distinguish between cause

[1] *Golden Bough*, vol. ii. p. 166.   The italics are mine.

and origin, purpose and effect, but he is really speculating on origin as well as cause, on purpose as well as effect, when he attributes the phenomena of Nature to the personal and voluntary action of sun or storm ; in fact he is thinking rather of origin and purpose, because the scientific idea of cause is a later development of thought. The scientific theory deals with causation only, for, as we have seen, origin and end are not accounted for by science, but are merely put outside the scientific region. They are not therefore outside the limits of human speculation, but are rather essential parts of the whole aspect of the universe to the human being.

But again, are natural science and religion dealing even with the same experiences? The evolution of science is through the testing and rejection of hypotheses inadequate to account for developing experience. Of what kind are these experiences? Are they experiences of natural phenomena or of spiritual phenomena, of growth of crops and fruitful showers, of succour in war, or of inward spiritual growth and fruitful sorrows, of help given against warring passions and selfish isolating impulses? The argument that religion is superseded by science may be true if religion means no more than this—"a propitiation or conciliation of powers superior to man which are believed to direct and control the course of nature and of human life" and if "a conscious or personal agent," whose "conduct is in some measure uncertain, . . . can be prevailed upon to vary it in the desired direction by a judicious appeal to his interests, his appetites or his emotions."[1]

If the central conception of religion is that man desires to make use of the Deity to irrigate his land or multiply his herds, then the scientific water-wheel is superior to the prayer-wheel, and a devout congregation is merely the elaboration of a super-stitious way of producing well-folded flocks.

But this view of religion is the most rudi-mentary and material; it is not certain that the most elementary form of religion is thus barren of spiritual qualities; and if any one would prove that the spiritual aspirations of later religion develop from such a germ they must be latent within it, for it is on spiritual lines that the "growing experiences" develop. And such a definition of even elementary religion seems not inadequate only, but even false to the thirst for God which begins in the simplest aspiration after purity and love, and which expands in the devo-tion of the saint and the bliss of the mystic.

[1] *Golden Bough*, vol. i. p. 63.

C. PARALLELISM OF CHRISTIANITY AND OTHER RELIGIONS—*Continued*

CHAPTER XII

EVOLUTION AND REVELATION

But it may be said : " Such a view of the evolution of religious ideas does away with any idea of religion as a divine revelation, or of Christianity as a unique divine revelation. Religion is made to be merely the human theory of the nature of the universe ; what truth there may be in it is mixed with error, it is arrived at by the gradual rejection of erroneous theories, and at no stage can we say, this is now really true. The whole idea is absolutely opposed to the idea of a revelation made to man by God."

But what do we mean by a divine revelation ?

Divine revelation has sometimes been conceived as a kind of compendium of necessary truth given to certain men who were bound to proclaim it to others. It was painful to our fathers to part with the belief that the very words of the message were dictated ; similarities between

" natural " and " revealed " religion were explained
by the assertion that legends, rites, and doctrines
of natural religion were "types" or "foreshadow-
ings" of the true revelation, as if Divine Power
had arranged these resemblances like a series of
tableaux vivants of the living truth, not as if they
had been produced by any natural law.

But if we try to translate that which is fundamental and essential in the theory of revelation
into our modern conceptions and terms, what do
we arrive at ?   The idea of natural law has, as
we have seen, in other regions superseded the
forensic idea of law as direct fiat ; yet natural
law is not incompatible with personal action.
The newer conception of Nature as embodying a
Divine Idea and being the result of a Divine Will,
is no more self-contradictory than the old conception of Nature as controlled from the outside by a
Personal Will ruling alien matter.   And if there is
a Divine Reason, a word or wisdom of God creat-
ing the world, there will be no point at which we
can say, this is the world apart from the Divine
Reason.   If we believe this we cannot say of
natural religion that it is due to the inventive
power of man apart from God, but we must conceive of it as the undeveloped idea beginning
to work itself out in human thought, and must
believe that the same Divine Reason which forms
the world works also in the first essays of the
human intellect.   If one and the same principle
is at work in the world and in thought, then

human thought, acting on the material given it in the world, considering light and darkness, life and death, good and evil, will, through inadequate endeavours, necessarily move gradually inwards towards the fundamental truth of existence, as it works outwards towards the true connection of phenomena with one another. Viewed under this aspect revelation is not in any way opposed to the human discovery of truth, and the primitive legends or truths do not present themselves as an arbitrary or arranged set of types of the truths of "revelation," but are like them simply because they are produced by the same inherent law ; man's religious "inventions" are not opposed to God's revelations, but man's discovery and God's revelation are two sides of the same process.

In fact, the idea that the evolution of religion affords any presumption that the developed result is untrue, is in reality based on the same separation between man and Nature which in other regions is not only untenable in itself but creates unnecessary difficulties. If we are looking at man from the purely natural side we shall see that his thought must be evolved on the same lines as his whole existence is evolved. Ultimately then thought and its manifestation cannot part company.

But it may be said that just as in Nature the process of "selection" is a process of rejection, as "out of fifty seeds" but one may be brought to bear, so science is evolved by the rejection of inadequate hypotheses. Like the sheath of a flower the inadequate hypothesis holds the expanding idea until such time as it is strong enough to bloom, and the sheath falls or dies away. Therefore there is nothing in the mere fact of evolution to show whether that which has been developed is truth which will endure, or error which will presently be rejected.

This is quite true. The method is no criterion of the objective truth of the result. The fact that astrology and astronomy were both "man-made" systems does not prove that either is a merely fanciful system, neither does the fact that they have both been brought about in the course of the development of human thought prove their objective truth. Yet we hold that the objective truth of one and the falsity of the other have been proved. How is this?

Astronomers have not brought nearer the objects with which their theory deals. Mars and Jupiter are just as far off as before, but whereas it became more and more evident that the star theories of astrology were inadequate to the facts, so astronomy has been able more and more to expand its radically right star-theories, and to embrace in a consistent scheme the growing mass of *star experience.*

Even so the truth of religion cannot be proved or disproved simply by the question of its method of development. If method were to be made the criterion, it is plain that there is nothing to tell us whether any one religion is not a mere imperfect stage—one of the fifty seeds which will not be brought to bear. But we need to know if the theories which we call religious doctrine can progressively embrace the growing mass of spiritual experiences.

It may be said that this conclusion relinquishes any idea that Christianity is a unique or final revelation, or anything more than one of a number of religions, perhaps a little truer than the rest. Our generation in its youth encountered the same difficulty in another region of "evolution." "If man is the brother of an ape he cannot be a spiritual being." Physical evolution is no longer a difficulty to the believer in Christianity, nor a weapon in the hand of its assailant. But it is somewhat strange that many even of those who do hold a religion of which the keystone is the Divine Incarnation, should be so peculiarly anxious to divide the divine from the human as to demand an absolute gulf between natural and divine revelation. As in the former case the difficulty was caused by the arbitrary division between man and Nature, so in this case the difficulty is caused by as arbitrary a separation between the divine and the human. If the truths which find their fullest expression in Christianity have a human history, why is the Christian revelation therefore less divine? If the human and divine were thus incompatible then also the Son of God must be proved not divine because he was the son of Mary.

In fact, there are two different senses in which Christianity as the absolute religion can be distinguished from other religions. In the first sense revelation is placed in opposition to natural religion, for the seeking of man after God is arbitrarily separated from the revelation of God to man. If we believe that natural religion is the history of man's futile attempts to discover something about God, but that revelation must be an announcement to man of some truths wholly disconnected from anything which he can discover, then indeed the similarities between Christianity and other religions would show that Christianity was neither unique nor final and no true revelation. This view finds no support in Scripture, and yet it is attacked and defended as if it were the "orthodox" view.

But in the scriptural sense Christianity is the revelation of an absolute relation between God and man, and therefore is the completion of partial revelations made at different times throughout the world's history.[1] In this sense it is both unique and final, and just because it is final it is the basis of fuller unveiling by a Spirit which will lead all who receive It into more truth; for if this absolute relation is a fact, it implies that man may be the subject of infinite revelations of the infinite nature of God. There is no opposition

[1] Cf. Acts xiv. 17; xvii. 22 ff.   Rom. i. 19, 20; ii. 14, 15.

between the unique revelation of Christianity and the continual revelation from the God who is not far from every one of us.

The further question whether indeed any religion is "final" in this sense, is a question which cannot be judged from the method of its development but from its adequacy to experience.

CHAPTER XIII

§ 1. BEFORE we proceed briefly to review the difficulties which we have arrived at from the scientific and historical point of view, let us notice that even during our own generation these difficulties have shifted their ground.

The enquirer in Browning's *Easter Day* exclaims—

> How comforting a point it were
> To find some mummy-scrap declare
> There lived a Moses!

But now when the cities of Raamses and Pithom are discovered, or the name of Israel is found on an Egyptian monument, only an archaeological interest is aroused; for inaccuracies in the Old Testament history of Israel in Egypt would no longer be a stumbling-block in the way of Christian belief, and the confirmation of a detail would bring no special " comfort."

Again, in the region where scientific difficulties were once rife, there is an increasing belief both popular and scientific in the power of mind over matter; and the practical popular beliefs in cures not produced by physical means, whether attributed to the Virgin at Lourdes or produced by the teaching of the Rev. Mary Baker G. Eddy in America, have become a subject of scientific investigation. The miracles of healing are no longer a serious difficulty, even the idea of resuscitation is not wholly out of reach of the scientific imagination.

Yet on the whole we cannot say that the evidence of science establishes our belief in Christianity; rather we must confess that, though science may have nothing to say against the fundamental belief in God, in the soul, in immortality, it is because these beliefs are entirely out of its sphere, and belong to another plane of thought; and that as regards the records of such events as do come into the sphere of its investigations, there are still many incidents of which science only can say that they are produced according to no known law, or even sometimes according to no imaginable law.

Again, we found that while historical testimony is fully adequate to establish the large outlines of Christian history, it is impossible to say that the historical testimony, even to the most important supernormal incidents, is so unimpeachable as to afford strict scientific evidence. Though criticism establishes much, much is thereby put in doubt. We may urge, on the other hand, that the science of historical criticism is only in its infancy, and that no certain conclusions can be based on a

study of style or of thought without a study of
the fundamental causes which underlie the historical record—namely, the *individual* characters
of the personalities which act and record, and that
finally any judgments of character must be insufficient without a real grasp of the unique character
and teaching which, in the case of Christianity,
so impressed the minds of recorders that the
results are lifted altogether out of the ordinary
plane.   Thus the historical criticism of the records
of Christianity cannot possibly be complete unless
it include, not only the study of character, but the
study of the power of religion itself.

But though history seems to prove that some
great disturbing power must have produced the
phenomena of Christian belief, the general history
of religions leads us to the question whether
Christianity itself is more than a kind of nervous
crisis in a stream of tendency ; for the comparative study of religions seems to show that the
rites, the narratives, and the fundamental ideas of
Christianity may be paralleled all over the world
by religions in different stages of development,
and suggests the conclusion that Christianity is
but one stage of a particular kind of human
thought, of which the whole tendency may possibly
be erroneous.

§ 2. Now no one really believes that *truths* are
contradictory ; nor consequently that religion can
be at variance with history and science except in

so far as one or other is false; and the realisation of apparent discrepancies between science and religion at any given time produces, on minds which do not wish to think much or to wait long, one of two effects.

Those who are not thoroughly interested in the scientific question and whose whole soul is in their religious belief, are inclined to say, "Where science has yielded so much, it may yield more, and may presently concede that there are modes of operation in which even such miracles as the multiplication or transmutation of matter may be brought about." This view has some practical strength, but those who stop here neither have nor seek to have any intellectual satisfaction.

On the other hand, those whose minds are impressed with the reign of law in Nature, and whose experience does not lead them to attach much value to religious belief, are inclined to say, "Where religion has yielded so much may it not yield more? Religious thought has been forced to allow that some miracles are unessential—that, for instance, the miracle of the stater in the fish's mouth is not a crucial point in the acceptance of Christianity—why should not the whole miraculous structure go, and leave us some useful ethical principles which need no longer be guarded and commended by the beauty of the legendary elements which once clustered round them?" Thus many conscientious and truth-seeking minds attempt to find what kernel of Christianity may be left untouched by doubt, and it seems to them that they cannot do better than accept the ethical teaching of Christianity wherever they find it adaptable to modern conditions; and that they may safely regard Jesus as first among the leaders of pure and spiritual thought even if they cannot accept the religious theory of Christianity, partly because they feel it impossible to be sure what Christ really said, and partly because they cannot feel certain that He knew more of the secret of existence than other men. Yet His general standard of conduct is their guide for life when other more directly practical guides fail, and from this acceptance of Christ's ethical teaching they gain a dim hope for death, a hope cherished since they have no other hope, but joyless because it is so dim. The position is in a sense impregnable because no one particularly wants to attack it. It is like holding a fortress in an uninhabited country or defending a barren rock in a great ocean.

But doubts even of this ethical basis sometimes arise. Are we sure that Christianity is so safe a guide to conduct? What proof is there that Christ's teaching was as true as it was beautiful? Is it even certain that we can consider it ethically sound? Do not let us compare it with our practice, which no doubt falls short of our aspiration, but let us compare it with our very standards of life. Christ's doctrine of self-sacrifice is hard to

reconcile with our gospel of self-development;
Christ's doctrine of forgiveness is not quite on the
same lines as our theories of reforming or deter-
rent justice; nor His doctrine of mercy with our
acceptance of natural selection and the survival
of the fittest; the teaching of the Man of Sorrows
stands in strange contrast with our present view
of the value of happiness. If an attack were
made on our position we do not feel certain it
would be so impregnable after all.

§ 3. But our preliminary review of the general
results of philosophic thought showed us the
inadequacy of so-called positive knowledge to
cover the field of rational human belief.

No discussion of the connection of phenomena,
no realisation of the way in which things came to
be, can tell us what they are in themselves. The
attitude of the human spirit to the universe is
much larger than that; it asks not only the
question "How?" but the question "Why?"
and the all-embracing question "What or Who?"

History and science yield us material for
philosophic thought which must take cognisance
also of other regions of experience. Let us then
turn to the constructive position, and leaving aside
for the time all the uncertainties with which we
have been dealing, let us simply ask "What is
meant by religious experience?" Religious
experience includes facts—actions and movements
—in the external world, but not these alone; it

includes also facts which have the same subjective existence as perceptions of beauty or feelings of admiration. Moreover, it is not only the nature of the facts with which it deals that distinguishes religion from science or from history, but the aspect under which they are viewed. If we look at science as potentially taking account of all phenomena both physical and mental, we shall see that it regards facts in a totally different way from that in which religion regards them.

The physicist may deal with the same pheno-mena of sound as the musician, but he deals with the mode of their production and the vibrations which are their physical cause. The physiologist may deal with their action upon the nerves and brain of the musician, may number and measure his hurried or lengthened breathings as the music affects him. They are all dealing with the same subject-matter but under wholly different concep-tions. So too the religious and the scientific man are both dealing with the infinite facts of the universe, but under wholly different aspects. Science deals with the production and connection of phenomena, but touches on no purpose or end in the whole. There is nothing in the scientific aspect of phenomena which can make anything in any possible way worth while; for even the idea of " worth " does not enter into the concep-tions of science, and thus the essential nature of everything which we care for is entirely outside it. Science can analyse the production of sound, and ignore the soul of music; it can show the cause of colour, and miss the joy of beauty; it can show the genesis of all manner of social institutions, and miss the heart of love; it may even find the conditions of life, but cannot ask what life is; it may "sweep the heavens with its telescope" and fail to find God.

Thus the evidence for religion must consist partly in the same facts which are dealt with by science and history, and partly in experiences which must remain peculiar to itself, until science and history have so spread over their limitless field as to take in all that is and everything which has occurred. But religion looks at these facts under a conception totally different from that in which history or science regards them. The main object of all knowledge in religion is not the phenomenal but that which lies behind phenomena. It is not how things happen which is of most importance, but what they are essentially, whence they are, and why they happen—their meaning, their end, and their value.

Life and worth—that which is good, and some one for whom it is good—these are the two things of greatest importance in rational human life, and it is to these existences that we must now turn for evidence of religion.

We cannot make an exhaustive examination of "the good"; for our present purpose we must confine ourselves to that one determination of the good which we call righteousness or morality, and we must ask what religious belief is implied in the very existence of morality.

But "the good" has no existence apart from some one *for whom* it is good. Behind the abstractions of science, behind the personal manifestations and actions of history lies the great fact of Personality, the core and centre of existence. How far shall we find that somewhere in the mystery of Personality lies the whole solution of the problem ?

PART III

CONSTRUCTIVE

INTRODUCTORY

CHAPTER I

THE NATURE OF POSITIVE EVIDENCE

THE fact that man reasons to the existence of God does not essentially affect the question whether mankind came first to believe in God by direct inspiration or through a natural development of thought.

We may divide the evidence which constitutes the basis of this rational belief in God into three main classes :—

(1) The existence of powers, objects, and catastrophes of the external world ;

(2) Moral ideas and the consciousness of moral obligation ;

(3) The perception of personality.

Too little is known about the history of religion to make it possible to say that man begins to reason from one class of facts before another ; for instance, that he accounts for thunder as the voice of a god before he is capable of recognising some kind of moral obligation and

179

thinking of it as the command of a Supreme Being. Indeed, in the development of thought, we do not find these three classes of ideas following one another in chronological sequence. From the first the idea of personality pervades all man's conceptions of Nature. It seems probable that ideas of these three kinds are present before man begins to think about the existence of God at all. All our children receive their knowledge of God by revelation given through their teachers; but instruction would have no effect on the child unless there were something within to which it corresponded,[1] and it is this internal correspondence which is developed by fuller consciousness into what we call the rational basis of his belief.

When the living creature begins to be conscious of its relation to the world, the distinction between the animate and the inanimate has still to be learned, whether by the human child or the higher animal; for the kitten, like the child, deals with its toy as if it were living; and the less-developed races of men never arrive at a clear distinction between the personal and the impersonal. The interesting case of Mr. Hanna has lately given a luminous instance of the redevelopment of consciousness.[2] After a complete loss

---

[1] The notes of Helen Keller's teacher on this point are valuable. She was asked how she taught her deaf and blind pupil to understand the names of abstract ideas, for instance of the idea of love. She replied that it would be impossible to teach her unless the idea were in the child's mind. Her task was to teach her how to fit on to the feeling she had the expression of it in language.

[2] *Multiple Personality*, Sidis and Goodhart, p. 83 ff.

of memory caused by an accident, Mr. Hanna woke with a mind like a new-born child, and had to learn to distinguish himself from the outside world; and again, to distinguish the animate from the inanimate in a world which he at first regarded as entirely personal.

Thus it appears that in the development of consciousness, the recognition of personality proceeds side by side with the recognition of an external world; and by the time man begins to think of God at all, he has recognised personality though he may not have defined its limits.

It is probable, in the same way, that the germ of moral obligation began to exist before man became man, and therefore that it is latent in the human mind from the beginning. Not only the nurture, but still more the training given by the higher creatures to their young, implies a degree of responsible altruistic action; and, among the gregarious creatures, we find not only differentiation of social functions, but sometimes a rudimentary social code, the breach of which is penalised: while in the case of the animals whom we ourselves have trained, we find we can develop a sense of guilt, not only a fear of punishment, and a conscience which responds even more to approbation than to material rewards.

Of course the definite language which we must use to express such things is liable to give an impression of clearer consciousness than is perhaps the case; but we can hardly resist the conclusion that we may trace the beginnings of the moral sense even in the lower creation.

Thus, once we find among the higher animals the idea of personality and rudimentary ideas of obligation (which in some cases is discerned as emanating from a higher will), it is not a great assumption if we take for granted that among the most primitive men, these ideas were still more developed than among the highest animals we know. Whether or no primitive man received some direct revelations of a higher will[1] is a question which we cannot here prejudge; but, apart from direct revelations and experiences, the evidence for religious belief consists of the consideration of the powers and forces of external nature, of moral ideas, and of personality. These elements of evidence, so far as we can see, are always present.

We do not propose to examine the first kind of evidence at all. The proofs of the existence of God based on a consideration of the external world have been frequently dealt with, and are too familiar to need summarising here. Whether or no such proofs are ever cogent must be left to the individual judgment; and we have already

[1] Even as our animals receive from us direct revelations of a higher will, so may primitive races of man have had a "covenant ordained" to them, a revelation made through the means of the "ministering spirits" by whom they are surrounded. Cf. Heb. i. 14, ii. 2; and Gal. iii. 19. These passages of course are a religious interpretation of the only history with which the writers were familiar; but religious philosophy cannot limit religious interpretation to the history of the Jews only, but must extend the same principle to all history.

dealt with some of the difficulties in the way of religious belief which arise from the consideration of the external world. We have touched too, and shall touch again, on the connection of fundamental Christian beliefs with some great world-principles.

At present we pass on to consider the facts of the moral consciousness as evidence of religious belief.

A. THE MORAL DEMAND

CHAPTER II

THE MORAL IDEAL AND MORAL OBLIGATION

LET us see then what is meant by moral evidence, or, to put it another way, what the existence of moral ideals involves.

It must be noticed that we do not assume the existence of a moral state of things in the world, of people acting mainly according to the dictates of their consciences, but only the undeniable existence of ideals of morality, of moral obligation dimly recognised perhaps and partially responded to.

The very possibility of morality implies a measure of free-will, a possibility of choice, however limited. As we have seen, the existence of this power of choice is not proved, but we have a direct intuition of it, and what science cannot disprove it is forced to ignore. The idea of causation is based on it, and it is implied in the most rudimentary conception of morality.

It is probable that man is from the beginning

not without some consciousness, however dim, of right and wrong, and it has been shown by students of religions as primitive as those of Australian aborigines that there is reason for thinking that the earliest idea of a Supreme Being is the moral idea of a Being who will punish breaches of that which is held to be right.

But, although this question is of the deepest interest, it does not essentially concern our argument. The question with which we have to deal is, whether the very existence of morality is not itself an evidence for the existence of God.

The two essential facts of morality are the moral ideal and the sense of moral obligation— that is the belief in something not yet existing and the obligation upon us to make it actual.

Let us consider the ideal involved in such a familiar aim as the prevention of cruelty to children. When we look forward to the future of children, we contemplate an indefinite number of events, acts, and feelings which have not yet come to pass ; we see that all these may bear one of two characters, the character of kindliness causing happiness, or of cruelty causing suffering.

The moral ideal, that the acts shall be of the former character, lies wholly in the future; the moral obligation is the constraint upon all concerned that the future with its quite indefinite series of events, shall be determined in accordance with this ideal.

In this way the moral ideal, like every other

ideal, involves a reference to what does not yet exist and proceeds to make it exist: "The things that are not bring to nought the things that are." The ideal is the working power of something not yet embodied, a new beginning.[1] "Nothing, from a railroad to a cathedral," it has been said, "can be done without an ideal." We claim originative power—the power of bringing into existence that which is not in existence— whenever we say, "that was my idea," and even the claim that the idea was carried out by actual material means is really a plea of the same kind, namely, that the material lying everywhere about in the world was seized upon by an idea and made to become something which it was not.

> Consider it well: each tone of our scale in itself is nought ;
> It is everywhere in the world—loud, soft, and all is said :
> Give it to me to use ! I mix it with two in my thought,
> And, there ! Ye have heard and seen : consider and bow
> the head.

The Platonic theory that everything—"even hair and dirt"—has an idea, and that the idea is the archetype of the existing thing, we see to be true of those things which depend on human action.

Thus the moral ideal forces us to make a continual reference beyond the bounds of actual existence back to origination.

But the reference is not only backwards to the ideal as origin, but forwards. The facts of

---

[1] Some say that material conditions of brain, etc., *produce* the idea. This we have already discussed, but it does not really bear upon our point here, which is, that the idea of things not yet existing produces things which do exist.

existence seem continually to be in contradiction to our ideal. We have an ideal of justice— unrealised ; of happiness, untrue to the world as it is ; ideals of love and mercy, parodied by the facts of life. Yet slowly, partially, and with many backslidings, the world is gradually realising these ideals. Slow as their effect may be, small as their advance may seem, they are facts, and we cannot limit the possibilities of their advance nor the ultimate sphere of their action. Morality rises like a tide over the unmoral world, as life comes up over the inorganic.[1] We speak with rightful horror of the continuance of war, but if we compare the rules of civilised warfare, the treatment of prisoners, the respect shown to the bodies of the dead, the work of the Red Cross League, with the chained captives in the Roman galleys, the heaps of hands thrown down before the Pharaohs, the impaled bodies on Assyrian sculptures, we see that even through the evil of war the ideals are realising themselves, as blades of corn grow up through the bare soil of the field.

And the consideration of morality does not only force us to look backwards and forwards beyond the present, but to look through the surface of the present. What is meant by moral obligation ? What is implied in the very idea of obligation ? It is something which is not our own

---

[1] " From henceforth ye shall see the Son of Man coming," said Christ. Matt. xxvi. 64.

will, but to which our will is constrained to conform itself; something external, which our mind does not even always fully recognise at first; something which works out its own development as mind and will react on one another, the mind realising more fully the content of "the good" as the will conforms itself to its performance. But where then does that reside to which the will and mind have not yet conformed themselves, which has not yet been realised as an event or as a rule of conduct, that which is an originative force in the world, but which, not yet existing in the actual world, is being formed in it?

Thirty years ago men were content to talk of "a power not ourselves which makes for righteousness," and found it easier to think of this "power making for righteousness" than of a person willing righteousness. It was an abstract, incomplete idea, for the whole idea of righteousness is of something essentially existing in thought and will; an essentially spiritual existence, a spiritual, not a material power.

But can we attach any meaning to a spiritual power which is not a spirit? Do we really mean anything by "a power which makes for righteousness," if we do not mean a power which thinks and wills righteousness? Can we conceive of any power which thinks and wills which is not a personal power?[1]

---

[1] An abstraction is very often a convenient barrier which the mind erects to protect itself from confusion when we feel that our thinking is

Thus it seems that our consciousness of moral obligation and our experience of the effectiveness of the moral ideal, force us to recognise "a power, not ourselves, that makes for righteousness," and that we cannot think with any clearness or reality of this power except as a spiritual power, that is a Spirit.

beginning to lead us into regions beyond our reach.   But the abstraction is merely made in order that we may attend undistractedly to one or more qualities of a thing.   If we begin to treat the abstraction as a thing in itself, we shall find that it is unmeaning, *e.g.* in order to consider the quality of length, Euclid defines a line as length without breadth, but if we were to consider length without breadth as a thing in itself, because it is a simpler thought and is easier to understand, we should find that as a *thing*, it is unmeaning.   Thus "power that makes for righteousness," is a simpler thought than a person who makes for righteousness, for power is only one quality of a person.   But as *essential existence* it is unmeaning.

CHAPTER III

ARGUMENT FROM ACTUAL IMPERFECTION

§ 1. But as soon as we have argued from the fact of the moral consciousness and the recognition of moral obligation to the existence of a moral Being, the author and ruler of the world and the source of our moral consciousness, the old difficulty seems at once to come back with fresh force. If there is a supreme moral Being, how can it be that the creation seems so to violate all ideas of perfection and of goodness? If God is really good, how can we even for a moment actually stand in debate as to whether good or evil is the strongest power in the world? for the existence of all-powerful goodness ought to exclude, it would seem, even the faintest trace of imperfection in creation.

We must guard against one common fallacy here. The cruelty, the injustice, the imperfection, the suffering and sin of the world are often brought, so to speak, as charges against religion, and handled as if religion were responsible for their very existence; whereas, on the contrary, suffering exists as a fact whatever view we take of the world: and we can only speak of cruelty and injustice, of imperfection and of sin, in virtue of bringing into relation with the facts of the universe the ideals developed by humanity. These ideals on the one side, and the facts of the material universe on the other, can only conceivably be harmonised by some religious theory.

It is not religion then which creates the difficulty. On the contrary, it is in the direction of religion alone that the solution lies. The man who discards religion does not get rid of the suffering and imperfect world, nor of its contrast with his own ideals. He only gets rid of all hope of solution.

But any solution which comes from the side of religion is quite unsatisfactory unless it is based on a recognition of difficulties. Let us then present these difficulties in as clear and precise a form as possible. What do we really mean when we say that the course of the world itself is not moral, or that it does not seem to be justly governed?

We mean that we find in the world three things whose very existence seems irreconcilable with the idea of justice and perfection:—

(a) The existence of undeserved suffering;

(b) The existence of fruitless suffering;

(*c*) The existence of sin.

We should not regard the existence of suffering as an injustice if it were entirely compensated by result ; and if we take for granted the existence of sin, suffering would not be unjust if it were simply proportionate to punishment. On the contrary, our moral consciousness seems to suggest and approve an essential connection between sin and pain. Which of us would regard it as an evil that a man convicted of brutal cruelty should suffer, at any rate, so much pain as to make him comprehend what he had done, and be sorry for it ? But as a matter of fact, a very large part of the suffering of the world seems to be both unmerited and fruitless.

Let us consider what constitutes the sum of suffering, and we shall see what a vast part of it is apparently unmerited ; what a vast part of it seems to bear no relation at all to the sin of the individual nor even to individual transgression, ignorant or conscious, of the laws of Nature.

In the first place there is a vast sum of apparently accidental suffering, from the suffering of human beings caused by physical catastrophes— fire and earthquake, flood and famine—to the waste of animal life by things as unconnected with the lower creatures as these cosmic calamities are with ourselves—drought dealing death to myriads of living beings, war bringing slaughter and starvation to flocks and herds ; and beyond all this, there are all individual accidents which

we cannot number or sometimes even regard—
from the fly which gave us a sudden smart in
the eye and lost its own life thereby, or the
grasshopper we trod on and left half killed as
we walked across a summer field, to the child
crippled by some accident that no one could have
foreseen or prevented. But quite apart from
accidental suffering which is due to the dis-
harmony of cosmic elements, there is woven into
the whole fabric of creation vicarious suffering,
voluntary or involuntary, from the birth-pangs of
a mother down to the destruction of the drones
stung to death by the worker bees when their
function in the community is over. In many
ways and countless instances the parents suffer or
die for the children.

In these latter cases we seem to discern some
fruitfulness of suffering, some compensation for the
suffering by the result : that one individual should
suffer in continuing the family or race does not
appear perhaps so unmeaning to us, because
there seems to be a unity in the whole. The
loss of one part therefore we may think of as
compensated by the gain of the other ; the two
seem to be part of one whole, and the suffering
which appears fruitless when we regard the individual in abstraction from the whole, is compensated if we regard the individual in his true
relation to the whole. Indeed, when vicarious
suffering or self-sacrifice becomes voluntary, when
the unity, binding in one the sufferer and those

o

for whom he suffers, becomes realised in consciousness, even the suffering itself is transformed by means of this realised unity, which in plain language we call love.

It may be then that this clue, if we can hold to it, will lead us out of the difficulty we feel when we realise that sacrifice is the law of the world.

But the next point we arrive at seems to render our clue useless.

The sum of sacrifice in the world consists not only of the sufferings of certain individuals for the good of others who are closely connected by race or more consciously by affection, but of sufferings inflicted and sacrifices demanded by others of alien and hostile race, for the life of all creatures is sustained by the lives of others; the dying vegetation out of which the new grass springs, the sheep pasturing on the grass, and then slaughtered for human food; the human body attacked by the myriad infinitesimal hosts of disease which bring it to decay—this is a little picture of the whole. So entirely does life exist through the sacrifice of life that the attempt to avoid destruction of life is an absurdity, so little can it effect. The Indian fanatic with muslin round his mouth that he may not even breathe in a fly and thereby impiously destroy life, is a laughing - stock in the world which simply *could* not go on except through the sacrifice of many lives for one. Moreover this sacrifice of life is not merely a painless loss, but is accompanied by even fantastic forms of suffering.

Not only is this vast sacrifice of life for life always going on, but suffering accompanies the individual development of life. That suffering should accompany disease or injury is often spoken of as a beneficent warning that there is something out of order. "How many limbs," it is said, "might we not break without knowing it, how our bodies might be scarred, injured, and burned if blows and falls, rending and burning, did not hurt"; and we are told that the same beneficent power has made joy the concomitant of healthful life and energy. Yet even if this theory of pleasure and pain as guides to healthful or unhealthful modes of life were really accurate, still we should feel that an *omnipotent* beneficence might have set as the signposts of life joys sufficiently attractive to induce us to follow right ways securely, and thus have obviated the need of painful warnings.

Moreover the natural and necessary developments of life are not free from suffering. In body and in spirit we are fretted by our growing pains; if we hope therefore to find that suffering has its compensation at least in the strengthening development of powers and graces of character, we are constrained to confess that experience does not always confirm us in this view, but that we frequently see characters getting harder through painful experiences instead of more generous and more tender.

If then sacrifice and suffering seem to be part of the very constitution of the world, we cannot rest contented with the easy explanation that it is merely the punishment and remedy of sin. Even though suffering may be the result of sin, it is not apparently the effect of sin in a way which satisfies our sense of justice. And if it is indeed the result of sin, we are led on to the question whether sin is also woven in to the constitution of the world.

Before we can attempt to consider this, we must make clear what we mean by sin. If we mean merely intentional transgression of a law clearly realised, then indeed sin can only be possible to fully reasonable creatures whose will can choose or refuse the good ; but if the idea of sin is thus restricted we are left with another kind of imperfection to account for — namely, moral evil which is not sin. The distinction between sin and moral evil therefore, though useful for many practical purposes, is superfluous in this connection. Should we, for example, call jealousy sin or moral evil ? It is sin doubtless in the strictest sense, when it is clearly realised and deliberately indulged : but animals are fiercely jealous, and whether we choose to call this jealousy sin [1] or not, it is a grievous moral evil, causing

---

[1] Certainly if a baby of a day old can sin, as St. Augustine says, an intelligent dog can sin.

miserable suffering to the animal that feels it, and making it inflict physical evil on those who excite the jealousy. Yet this very jealousy seems to be a necessary accompaniment of the growth of self-consciousness by which the animal is gaining a higher plane in creation. Indeed we may regard it as the result of progress. The development of egotism, of which jealousy is a symptom, appears to be at once a necessary stage of progress and the root of that alienation from God which is the essence of sin.

When we speak of progress it must be remembered that we are at present living in a condition of profound ignorance; that our senses are only open to a very small part of the sense impressions which are streaming past us, and that our minds are little able to interpret even that which our senses can receive. As the new-born baby lies with open eyes and ears, blind and deaf to the impressions which are all around it, so we are blind and deaf even in a universe which is pouring itself forth in light and colour, in sound and scent, in infinite unknown variations every instant—

> The secrets of the gods are from of old,
> Guarded for ever and for ever told ;
> Blabbed to all ears and published in a tongue
> Whose purport the gods only can unfold.

It seems as if in this world only rare souls can ever for an instant stand in the naked light, and such souls cannot utter what they saw or heard.

"I was caught up and heard unspeakable words which it is not lawful for a man to utter," says one. Thus as we progress out of this state of profound ignorance and darkness, and one truth after another emerges into consciousness, it is not surprising if each thing we grasp is for the moment out of proportion to the rest, and this disproportion brings a want of harmony into the mind and soul, for a strife has begun. It is this strife which we seem to see when, through their love for us, the lower creatures apprehend something of our ideas or emotions : they, like ourselves, have to learn what is meant by individual life, and learning this, it appears that we necessarily realise our own individual wants, aims, desires, and desire them out of proportion to the whole.

Ultimately we begin to perceive that the satisfaction of our own desires would leave us yet empty, with leanness in our souls ; that the fullest development of individual life, even if it were possible for an individual to develop alone, would be empty and barren ; and so we begin to realise that the individual is what he is in consequence of his relation to others. Yet it would not be possible for most of us to rise out of our ignorance without passing through the stage of egotism.

Jesus Christ indeed appears never to have viewed His individuality in isolation—"I and the Father are one." Some will say this was because of His divinity; others, that in this lay His divinity; and others again, that this saying represents the highest point of spiritual achievement in the most spiritual human soul.

But though each of these explanations may represent one aspect of truth, still it appears as if humanity as a whole could not have attained this apprehension of a unity which embraces individuality except by passing through a stage in which individuality was realised in isolation—that is, the stage of egotism and alienation.

May we therefore regard sin as a necessary stage in progress? If so, it is, like suffering, inherent in the constitution of the world, and we are met by the double difficulty of believing in the benevolence of a Creator who could make a world in which suffering was not only an accident or an unavoidable consequence of sin, but a world of which sin and suffering were constituent elements. Could such a God be merciful or even just? Can we believe in Him as the moral ruler of the world?

Let us go back to reconsider what we mean by justice. The moral idea is not a simple indivisible thing—it is a thing of parts; it contains purpose; it implies an unfolding in time—so that one cannot divide a moral act or a moral idea and ask whether one part or another is moral *in itself*. The very ideas of justice, of punishment, of pardon, of hope, imply a relation of persons and acts or of intentions, and imply a process which we cannot understand except under the idea of time. Purpose, for instance, implies a beginning and an end, a process, a personal and an impersonal idea, a worker and his means of production, and, a final term, the realisation of the purpose through the means. So justice implies a right or wrong between at least two people, and the final realisation of the right.

If we then arbitrarily separate any one of these ideas from the rest, we cannot possibly find in the part so separated the complete moral idea ; and as all parts are essential, the moral idea is not there at all. The agent without the material, the material without the agent, both without an end for which they are combined, cannot exhibit the idea of purpose ; and the mere point at issue without any persons or final realisation of the right cannot display justice.

When we ask therefore whether the universe is moral, we must consider the universe as a whole ; it would be meaningless to separate the natural universe from man with his moral ideals struggling to gain gradual realisation. We must frame our question on larger lines, and ask whether the total scheme of things, including nature and man, what has been and what is to be, is moral. And when we have thus put the question, we see from the nature of the case that we cannot answer it, for we know only an infinitesimal part of the universe ; and even if we knew all that the universe contains and conjectured all that is past, we still should know but a little part of the whole, for we should not know the future. Now if the moral purpose is a purpose that runs through the universe, it cannot be complete until the universe itself is complete—that is, until the universe-in-time comes to an end.

§ 2. We cannot judge whether the universe is moral or not, whether pain is undeserved or not, whether it is fruitless or not, and in effect we do not know *what sin is*,[1] while we are ignorant on three main points :—

(*a*) What the end is going to be ;

(*b*) What individuality is ;

(*c*) How far time changes the qualities of things.

(*a*) The consideration of morality, of moral ideals and moral obligation, leads us straight out of ourselves and our present condition, for it implies a relation between ourselves and something outside us which is not yet made actual. But if we take merely a part of that which has become actual and question whether that isolated part is moral, the reply is neither yes nor no, for the question is meaningless, as meaningless as if we ask whether a green leaf is green in itself,

---

[1] Cf. Julian of Norwich: "And after this I saw God in a Point . . . by which sight I saw that He is in all things. I beheld and considered, seeing and knowing in sight, with a soft dread, and thought, *What is sin?* For I saw truly that God doeth all-thing . . . and I was certain He doeth no sin. And here I saw verily that sin is no deed : for in all this was not sin shewed " (*Revelations of Divine Love*, ch. xi.).

apart from the light by which it is seen and the eye which sees it. We cannot even know the moral of a book unless we read it to the end, for it may be that the consummation of the whole will reveal to us an altogether new conception without which this problem could not be solved.

(*b*) And again it is vain for us to reason from our conception of individual suffering when we understand individuality so little. Whether the individual is a complete existence in himself is a question which occurs in many ways to minds of different men and nations. The Indian doctrine of Karma is an attempt to explain all suffering as deserved, by the theory that a man suffers in one life for what he has done in a previous incarnation, though he has no memory of that former life. But such entire absence of memory would mean a different consciousness—in effect, a new man ; so that one can only consider the two lives as two separate individuals, united by nothing but the simple fact that the second bore the penalties or received the gain merited by the first ; and this is no more and no less "just" than any other case in which one man receives the reward of the good or ill deeds of another.

But is one individuality really a complete unity in itself and completely separated from others ? We have already referred to the case of Mr. Hanna. Before his complete recovery he had alternations of personality. In the one condition he had all the memories that belonged to his life before the accident, in the other the memory only of that which he had experienced subsequent to it. His friends took pains to give the one self the completest possible news of the other self, and whenever he emerged into the first condition he was encouraged to struggle against the return of the younger self. But the struggle was so intense that he felt it to be unbearable, and at the crisis found his choice lay between either giving up any aspiration after his earlier life or accepting both strands of consciousness as equally himself. He determined to accept both personalities, and carefully learnt all that was necessary to make the memories of the one life fill up the gaps left in the consciousness of the other. From that time he alternated no more and discarded neither of the two threads of life. It appears from these and other similar psychological observations, that there can exist in us two distinct threads of memory, emotion, and character which are not mutually conscious of each other; and Mr. Hanna's case proves that after the two have been separated they can be again reunited. If this is a matter of experience, it is not then unthinkable that a group of human beings in a family, a group of men in a nation or a church, indeed the whole race of man and conscious beings, can be part of a larger self; so that what we call individuality might be only a temporary, apparent, and felt isolation of some one thread of memory, sensation, emotion, and will. We know there are such diverse threads of thought and feeling in ourselves ; tendencies hostile to, and even destructive of one another ; is it not possible that there is a larger unity of which individualities are but separated strands of thought or even of feeling ? It is difficult to understand how creatures of a low degree of consciousness can be even as independent as we ourselves ; in order to account for the very existence of some phenomena which we observe in them, it seems necessary to postulate more than their own dim, blurred consciousnesses.

Let us take a very simple instance. A chicken came out from the egg so malformed that it was necessary to kill it. It is not perfectly easy to kill a newly - hatched chicken, and the mind of the killer revolted against the deed, feeling the cruelty involved in the creation of a creature so soft and tender which lived only in order that it might suffer and die, and had not one moment of pleasurable life. But when the chicken was dead the slayer began to reflect that the consciousness of such a creature is very rudimentary. It is questionable whether it had any conscious suffering, certainly it could have no memory of it. The intensely conscious spectator who killed the chicken to shorten this suffering probably suffered much more than the chicken. The sensation, the root and cause of the pain, appeared to be in the chicken; but the consciousness of it to be all in the spectator. Suffering here seems to be strangely distributed.

Now let us suppose that in handling the chicken the spectator's hand was torn by a bramble, and that the wound were discerned by some intelligent creature too limited in mere size and power of observation to realise the connection of brain and finger; the compassion of such a creature would be all directed to the finger where the sensation originated, not to the consciousness of which the seat was out of sight, but where the hurt was really both felt and known. Does anything analogous take place in the case of a creature with undeveloped self-consciousness, whose half-conscious suffering is realised not by itself, but by some more developed mind?[1]

(c) In effect then we find we know very little about individuality when we think of it as in any way isolated or independent. Perhaps we understand time even less. There is a tendency in modern philosophy to overlook the importance of time; to claim that imperfection or suffering in the past is as imperfect as imperfection in the present. Now this denial that time produces any change in quality is totally in opposition to direct feeling and experience which is to the

---

[1] Cf. this with the mystical presentation of Christ, "impossible," in so far as He is glorified, but possible in His members still upon earth. Is this spiritual imagination of the mystic really an intellectual perception of a higher order?

effect that present bliss is even heightened by the remembrance of past pain :

> Sleepe after toyle, port after stormie seas,
> Ease after warre, death after life does greatly please.

But present happiness is admittedly clouded by the expectation of pain in the future. The dentist behind and the dentist before us has a very different effect upon our enjoyment. Conversely, past bliss has an added poignancy of sorrow, future bliss a greater radiancy of happiness.

Many would question whether anything analogous can be said of sin, whether the happiness of a converted soul is increased by the sense of how great a sin has been pardoned; yet our Lord said, "to whom little is forgiven the same loveth little," and St. Paul seems to draw a heightened sense of God's love, therefore a heightened bliss, from the very fact that he felt himself to have been the chiefest of sinners : so too "there is more joy in the presence of the angels of God" in heaven and among His lovers on earth over one sinner that repenteth than over ninety and nine who need no repentance. Certainly the prospect of sin to come would be destructive of happiness in a way that sin past would not.

Thus as the tinkling bell on a horse changes its note as a vehicle approaches, is opposite, or passes farther from us into the distance, so to human consciousness living under conditions of time, events change their quality or their intensity according as they are past or future.

It is often said that eternity is an everlasting "now" in which "was and is and will be are but is." But if eternity were a simple "now" it would be more limited than time. As Hegel points out, the true infinity does not exclude the finite. So the true eternity does not exclude the distinctions of time. Indeed, it seems more than probable that there is something in eternity that we do not at present understand and can in no way express even in thought.

§ 3. If then we cannot judge whether the world is or is not moral because we do not yet know what the result will be, because we do not understand what individuality is, nor what time is, of what use is philosophy? It merely ends in agnosticism.

It is evident that a great deal of philosophy does end either in doubt of religion or in doubt of philosophy itself—either in certainty of its methods and despair of any result, or in doubt of the methods themselves. But is this perhaps the result of misconceiving the object of philosophy?

What do we conceive philosophy in this sense to be? Plainly, a theory of the universe; not of the material universe alone, nor of the psychological universe alone, but of those ethereal yet embodied existences also which we call art and religion.

Do we then expect our philosophy to be a complete and definite scheme of the universe, or do we expect it to be an indication of certain great lines of truth which go on into infinity?

We may illustrate these two conceptions of philosophy by two maps successively made of a buried temple, one by French, the other by English excavators. The French turned the ground up here and there; found here a door, there a chamber, here the beginning of a colonnade, and joyfully planned out a symmetrical temple. The English excavators cleared the whole ground plan, mapped out every foundation they could discover, wall and pillar and statue, and indicated what had probably existed by dotted lines. When compared the maps were not much alike, for that which was completed on a French view of symmetry was found not at all to correspond with the facts of the disinterred foundation.

But our temple of the universe is partly buried under the dust and sand of epochs past; it soars up into the skies beyond our measurement, and away from us stretch great cloisters and colonnades into darkness, with dim statues whose faces we cannot clearly descry: and our philosophy cannot possibly be true if it maps out the universe as though it were all in sight and could be measured in its actual proportion. We can but indicate its general plan, not exactly measure its length and breadth and depth and height.

A. THE MORAL DEMAND—*Continued*

CHAPTER IV

EXISTENCES IMPLIED IN MORALITY

§ 1. WE must remember that although we have spoken of the moral ideal as being something not yet fully realised, yet that this moral ideal is just as much a fact in the universe as the existence of any natural object—a stone or tree—a fact indeed far more powerful in its effects than most material things, for that which is in a sense visionary is not therefore ineffectual. The repentance which has built a cathedral is no less a fact than the stones and mortar of which the cathedral is made; and if the cathedral, as a great architect once said, "brings people to their knees," it is because a sense of the Divine framed mere stones and mortar into a language which speaks out their inspiration to human hearts.

We have seen in the previous chapter that the very existence of moral ideals and moral obligation points to something outside the natural course of the world, to a beyond—present, past, and future.   Though moral ideals are facts, yet in so far as we look only on what has been realised in the world, there is an incompleteness about them. The system to which they belong is not yet developed.   Thus the moral world is not a wholly different world from the physical world, but a world inclusive of the physical, and physical facts take new proportions in it, and a new aspect. They do not form, as in natural science, the whole material to be correlated ; they are only a part of the whole, and they are only of importance in relation to feeling and to conduct.   Our idea of justice may be called visionary, but the solid physical facts involved in the execution of justice —the murder, the apprehension, the jury and the judge, the death of the condemned criminal—are all a special grouping of facts under this conception ; it is justice which has built the prison wall and raised the scaffold.   The physical facts gain their importance and derive their very existence from the "visionary" concepts.   So the whole view of the world as moral implies that it is not only a collection of physical things, governed by physical law, reasonable, and capable of being understood by reason, but that these physical things are part of a moral scheme, of a world in which moral ideas are active forces.

What then are the principles, the laws hidden from observation but open to reason which are necessary to form these facts into a moral system ? Kant summed up the assumptions which were needed to render the moral world a coherent whole, as God, the soul, and immortality. Our idea of justice, for instance, demands that right doing shall bring happiness, but since in this life such justice miscarries, we need to believe in an immortal life in which the perfect justice of God may be worked out.[1]

If then these assumptions are necessary to morality as an ordered system, are we justified in treating them as established truths ?

Now we saw earlier that the whole coherence of physical facts as a scientific system depends upon the assumption of a principle which we can never observe in external nature — the law of causation. Unless everything had a cause, and unless the same cause always produced the same effect, there would be no system in Nature but a mere chaos. We cannot observe the actual causal link in things outside us, and we cannot prove by simple observation that the same cause always produces the same effect, for it often appears to be otherwise. Nevertheless, if we steadily hold to this principle in the face of apparent failure our system becomes coherent.

This is a legitimate process in science ; in fact, it is only through these assumptions that science

---

[1] It is interesting to notice in this connection the development of belief in immortality among the Jews. Through disheartening experience the pious Israelite clung to the idea that God rewarded righteousness and punished the ungodly in this life ; and it needed the stress of religious persecution to compel him finally to the hypothesis of a future life to which other less spiritual nations had earlier attained.

exists. Is it not therefore also legitimate, if we take a moral view of the world at all, to assert as true that which we must necessarily assume when we regard morality as a coherent system ?

In the physical world we assume the same reason as we find in our own mind. In the moral world we have an equal right [1] to assume a wisdom which works for an end, and that end good. We ourselves have an idea of an end, a goal to which all things work ; an idea of final good is implied in all our moral action ; we have a right then to assume in the universe this same principle of wisdom, infinitely larger and more originative than human wisdom, even as the reason in the universe is greater and more creative than the human reason.

[1] It may be urged that we have not the *same* right to assume the truth of our moral as of our intellectual principles : for we only want the latter to hold true of the phenomenal world of our experience, made up of our perceptions. But what chiefly concerns us about our moral principles is to know if we have a right to apply them to a world which lies beyond our perceptions ; it is not enough to know that they apply to the world as it appears to us, though this *is* enough to know about our scientific principles. But we want to know if our moral principles will go on being true when the shadows of the world have passed away ; that they represent an eternal, not merely a temporal view of the world ; whereas it does not concern us to know if our scientific principles represent any distinct " absolute " truth. How can we then, on the same lines of reasoning, count the moral principles as absolutely true ?

The difference is not so great as it seems. We do need to apply our intellectual principles to a " beyond " before man was born on the earth and after he ceases to exist ; and in either case we believe that intellectual or moral principles will be true in the same measure in which we apprehend truth. Wherever we come across one and one in the universe, abstractly they will be two, and wherever we come across abstract justice it will be the same kind of justice that we know now.

§ 2. But it may be objected that moral facts can give us no sure basis of experience. It may be said that since morality is evolved it is still in process of evolution. If so, it is no use taking our present ideas of morality as fundamental facts because they may be completely altered by evolution.

But to say this is completely to misunderstand the nature of evolution, which is not a process of altering fundamental principles, but of carrying them out to their furthest results.

The evolution of morality could not possibly mean its fundamental alteration, but the following out of its fundamental principle into greater detail, as Christ's version of the Law was a development of the Commandments.

But it may be said : " This would be a sound argument if all men were agreed as to fundamental moral principles ; but moral principles vary from age to age and from nation to nation. What national morality shall we take as a standard, and at what period of history ? "

Now it simply is not true that fundamental principles of morality differ at different times and among different nations. The practice and habits may differ at different times and among different nations ; there may be immoral periods of history where morality is disregarded ; there may be un-moral periods, when a nation, like a child, is not old enough to understand, and a nation may possibly continue with a minimum morality like an

idiot or the lower kinds of animals ; but in so far
as nations own a morality the fundamental precepts are singularly alike, though they may have
different developments and circumstantial form.

The fundamental moral ideas of honesty, of
good faith, of generosity, of justice, of duty, of
courage, of self-sacrifice, of love, of temperance,
of purity, of obedience, of piety, remain from age
to age and nation to nation, though their application may alter and their proportion vary.

It may be that nations, like the Arabs at
present, recognise the obligation of honesty or
faithfulness only towards their own friends, and
consider it a thing to be proud of to cheat or
thieve and lie on their behalf; that some recognise the duty of faith, generosity, self-sacrifice
towards guests in what appears to us a dispro-
portionate degree, and repudiate any such duty
where we consider it indispensable ; yet however
limited the application, the core of the virtue is
still always the same, and the evolution is in the
line of extended application, or of more careful
definition of the proportionate importance of
different principles in a conflict of duties.

We are tempted to exclaim "how modern!"
when Ptah-hetep, of four thousand years ago,
charges us to avoid bad temper, "for when a
man takes Justice for his guide and walks in her
ways there is no room in his soul for bad
temper"; [1] or to say "how advanced!" when

[1] *The Maxims of Ptah-hetep, XIIth Dynasty.*

Mr. Andrew Lang shows us the Australian aborigines condemning the selfish person as the "uninitiated."[1] It is not really modern nor advanced, because it is neither old nor new, but eternal.

But again it may be urged that morality is not a fundamental fact of the universe, since it has come into being comparatively late and as a mere idea of the human species; it only begins to exist as a result of the higher development of consciousness.

This fact does not render the idea of morality any less fundamentally true however, nor any less an essential element of the universe as a whole. We do not prove that moral ideas are fanciful and purpose a figment because they do not come into actuality until the higher stages of evolution are reached. It is the last term of a development, not the first, which interprets the whole. If we separate the creation from man we find indeed that it is morally imperfect; but it is this separation, this limitation, which is still at fault. Man, and the thoughts of man, his moral ideas as much as his consciousness or even his body, are on one side part of Nature and the result of the evolution of the universe.

Thus for the present argument we do not need to reckon with the origin and growth of morality, nor the permanence or universality of definite moral principles; the experiences which we have

[1] *The Making of Religion*, p. 235.

taken as a basis are the simple facts of the distinction between good and evil, the existence of moral ideals, and the recognition of moral obligation.

§ 3. If for the existence of morality the ideas of God, the soul, and immortality are necessary, for the actualisation of morality another assumption is essential, namely, the existence of power to fulfil the moral law.

The moral law is in a sense external to the soul; it is a word from outside, for it is as much affirmed by the man who disobeys it as by the man who obeys it. When a man pursues evil with the consciousness that it is evil, he recognises something which is in opposition to his will and his pleasure no less clearly than when he sacrifices his pleasure to choose the good. In disobeying, as much as in obeying, he assents to the law that it is "holy and just and good." But it is not until his will is what Kant calls "a holy will," that is, utterly identified with the law, that the law ceases to be in some sense external.

But how can this externality be overcome? Man's natural will is not identified with the law : how has he power to conform himself to it ?

Two answers have been given to this question by the great religions and moralities of the world. On the one hand, it is affirmed that man[1] can

---

[1] If not the individual man, at any rate the race of men gradually working upwards : or the individual man through successive reincarnations.

by his own effort ultimately conform his will to the law of righteousness ; on the other, that man can only conform himself to the law of righteousness through power imparted to him by God.

Thus Buddhism teaches that this possibility of perfect holiness can be worked out by human kind. Through successive transmigrations the Buddha Gautama worked out his Karma, and entered upon a state void of emotion or desire or any of the active and disturbing elements of life —that state of being which is nothingness. And this attainment is theoretically possible to all men : indeed no other end than Nirvana is possible ; but by what power any soul with an increasing Karma of evil habit can take the first upward step is unexplained. If a downward path is once begun each successive life must begin at a worse advantage, and there is no doctrine in Buddhism of an external power which can make a man's burden, like Christian's, roll off his back, and set him strengthened on his upward way.[1] Man must work out his own salvation, but there is no "God who works in him to will and to do."

This difficulty in Buddhism is a difficulty in all forms of religious belief, under whatever name they appear, which place man with his simply natural powers, tainted and diseased as we know them to be, face to face with the law of perfection.

In opposition to this we have the answer of

---

[1] There are of course teachers or masters of different degrees who will help by discipline and instruction.

Christianity, which is echoed by many God-seeking souls of all ages and creeds, that it is impossible for the tainted human soul to renew its own life ; that man needs redemption from past sin and the power of a divine life to enable him to rise to a life of righteousness.

The two answers which are given to this problem must in the ultimate resort rest on experience ; they will be given in all kinds of ways ; the Jew may dictate the words in which the Christian will entreat—

> Purge me with hyssop, and I shall be clean :
> Wash me, and I shall be whiter than snow.
> Create in me a clean heart, O God ;
> And renew a right spirit within me.

And pagan instruction, pagan sacrifice, pagan communion may bear witness to the same inner experience that redemption is needed, and the communication of a divine life is possible.

It is only such a belief which can bring comfort to those who, through the condemnation of society, have been brought to know their own extremity, or to those who have become conscious of weakness and possibilities of sin as fundamental if less manifested. But the impossibility of self-renovation may be less apparent but no less real for those who are so blinded by respectability that they comfortably believe they are going to leave the world better than they found it.

§ 4. If then redemption from sin is a demand

of the moral consciousness, is not there also a demand for redemption from the suffering and death which are so intimately and mysteriously connected with sin?

But if we simply believed that the time was coming when all suffering would cease to exist, that would not remove the contradiction between the moral ideal of perfection and the imperfection of the universe as we know it, for there would still remain the vast past of sin and pain.

Past sin and past suffering mar the perfection of the universe, though they do not mar it in the same way as present sin or suffering; to say this would be to deny the reality of any idea of process.

Process indeed is a thing belonging to time, but since it exists at all, it must exist in eternity; it cannot be annihilated by the expansion of time into eternity, for then the sin or suffering which has been "overcome" in the course of time and history would be equally prevalent with that which overcame it. If the earlier barbaric stages of the world were in time overcome, yet even though time itself should in a sense disappear, it cannot be so blotted out that eternity can be a "now" in which barbarism is still existent.

But though past evil is not the same as present evil, it is still a blot on perfection, unless in its relation to the whole it assumes some altogether different quality. The whole moral consciousness revolts against the idea of unjust or useless suffering ; but though much or even most of the suffering we see has the appearance of being un-merited or fruitless, yet we have found reason to suspect that our narrow and limited view of in-dividuality is not an absolute truth, and that therefore the justice of suffering is a deeper thing than we know, and the fruitfulness of suffering a wider thing than we can measure. Thus we find that it is unreasonable to rebel, if we take a sacrificial view of the universe, against suffering as unmerited and uncompensated.

Yet even so we are driven to ask why should life involve a process which is so imperfect ? Why should imperfect means be taken of arriving at an ultimate good ? How can suffering be the only means which omnipotent Love has at com-mand? We cannot tell ; but we know that all philosophies which do not recognise that there is a taint in the world prove themselves shallow and superficial. This is no difficulty raised by religion ; it is a difficulty in the world of experi-ence with which philosophy or religion has to deal, from which many philosophies and religions try in vain to escape, but which the Christian religion openly recognises, for it is no part of Christianity to minimise evil, or to call it "non-existent" or "negative." But while it cannot unveil the Eternal Perfection which it asserts, it may by partial revelation indicate the nature of this unveiling.

Let us see what it is that the moral consciousness demands in this respect for its complete satisfaction.

It would find complete satisfaction only in knowing that pain was the best and most perfect means to the most perfect end, and pain had, so to speak, another side than that which we see; that *as* pain, *as* evident evil, it could be redeemed so that we should see it as forming part of some perfect thing, and that it had only seemed evil because we viewed it in abstraction.

The keynote of Hegel's philosophy is found in the word "*aufgehoben.*" The meaning of "*heben*" is "to raise," and of "*aufheben*" "to take away"; but the meaning of "*aufgehoben*" is also "preserved." We find the unity of these two opposed ideas—"taken away" and "preserved"— in the idea of transformation; for transformation implies both continuity and change. Apply this conception here; in order to satisfy our idea of perfection the evil element must be "*aufgehoben,*" that is, it must be "taken away," for *as* pain or *as* evil it must exist no more, or the universe will be still imperfect; but it must be at the same time "preserved," that is, it must be transformed, so that its having been, and even its imperfection must be a part of supreme perfection.

If there is a power by which sorrow can be so tempered that it "reaches us like a solemn joy"; if we can "rise on stepping-stones of our dead selves to higher things," then there is such a transforming power in the universe, and it is this power which the moral consciousness demands.

§ 5. Let us then briefly see what conclusions we have reached through the consideration of the moral facts of the universe.

We have seen that it is as necessary for philosophy to take account of the facts of morality as of any other cosmic existences, and that philosophy cannot consider facts except as part of a system. Yet experience must recognise that the facts of morality are by themselves incomplete, and if they belong to a system they involve for their completion the existence of a spiritual power of righteousness which we cannot conceive as less than personal, and whom therefore we must call God.

Moreover, the moral demand for perfection must imply some justification of the incompleteness of justice here, some restitution of all things ; and the obligation of the moral law demands the existence of a power to fulfil it—a power therefore which can transform the evil which meets us in an immediate experience.

These are briefly the results we have arrived at, but we note that as we ascend into a higher region of things our argument involves more and more an element of choice.

Even when we considered the scientific facts of the universe we saw that the development of our philosophy depended on a sense of the value of certain ideas; we could fix our attention simply on the chain of causes and effects, and rest contented with the scientific explanation of the universe; but if origin and purpose seemed to us supremely important we must necessarily go beyond the limits of scientific thought.

Thus again, though we all must come across the existence of moral facts and ideas in the world, it may be that we do not all consider them of sufficient importance to reason that they must be parts of a complete moral system. Such a conclusion may reach our mind with no insistence; we even may class moral ideas with illusions and imagination, not with the fundamental forces of the world.

As we proceed we find that the element of choice must again appear, inasmuch as our experience of life is determined in one way or another by our desires, emotions, and actions. Whether a man thinks he is able by his own power to conform his will to the law of righteousness will evidently depend on the extent of his aspiration and failure, or his consciousness of failure.

Once more, we have said that though morality may vary, fundamental principles of morality remain the same.

But, as we have before indicated, it is possible to return on the track, and to deny the reality of moral obligation.[1] For there is a philosophy of

---

[1] This is quite distinct from transgressing moral obligations; the transgressor recognises and defies the obligations.

conduct which substitutes an ideal of self-development for a theory of duty, and it is obvious that the conclusions which are based on the conception of moral obligation will carry no conviction to a man whose ideal is primarily that of self-development.

It is impossible here to deal with the conclusions which would result if we followed out all these alternatives. It is enough to show that choice must necessarily play a part in our reasoning as we ascend from the world of externally determined facts to the universe of moral existence. Reason cannot remain a bare intellectual faculty; it must become a faculty of judgment dealing with the question of values.

B. THE SPIRITUAL REALITIES

CHAPTER V

TESTS OF SPIRITUAL EXPERIENCE

§ 1. But all this moral evidence for religion is indirect evidence : for our argument is based on the implications which are involved in the very existence of morality ; and we have shown how the assumptions which morality forces us to make may be compared to the assumptions of causation in the natural world.

But although we do not derive the conception of causation from external Nature, it is not an imaginary creation of the human mind, for we have immediate experience of causation in the action of our own wills. We probably first realise that we are ourselves and "other than the things we touch" when we realise that we can exert force.[1] It is in ourselves, not in nature, that we have the experience of productive power, which is then assumed to exist in external nature, and

---

[1] Cf. *Multiple Personality*, p. 102.

in virtue of which, Nature becomes to us a systematic whole and our knowledge of it becomes science.

Have we then in the same way any immediate experiences corresponding to the assumptions required by morality ; or is the indirect evidence of morality the only evidence we have of spiritual realities ?

It is undeniable that many people in all ages and professing many creeds have believed that they had such an immediate experience of spiritual realities ; and we shall presently have to enquire whether the nature of these spiritual realities corresponds to the moral demands. But we are first confronted with a preliminary question, namely, whether it is necessary that such experiences should be universal if they are to have the force of evidence.

It is clear that an immediate sense of spiritual existences is not an experience universally recognised. One cannot say that all men are conscious of spiritual experiences, as one can say that all men are conscious of determining their voluntary actions. Yet if the things experienced are realities and not the "subjective" results of individual imagination, why should they not be universally recognised ?

There are several ways of accounting for experiences which are asserted with conviction by a few, but unrecognised by the greater part of mankind.

In the first place, the supposed experience may be a delusion or a mistake. If a fever patient sees a figure where other people see none, it is probable he is under a delusion; or, even if several people assert that they have seen a sea serpent, and the majority of naturalists are sure that there is no sea serpent, it is probable that those who said they saw it were mistaken. They saw something no doubt, but that something was not a sea serpent; they misinterpreted their experiences. So there are many who assert that St. Paul was under a delusion caused by a sunstroke when he saw a vision and heard a voice, and that those who believe that they have been released by the Spirit of God from the power of the devil have experienced *something* no doubt, but misinterpret their experience.

But there are two tests which may be used to differentiate mistakes from delusions, and both from unusual experiences.

(*a*) The first is the extent and effect of the delusion.

If the person who believed that he saw a sea serpent also believed that he heard the sea serpent and that he felt the sea serpent collide with the ship he was in, the experience would not be a simple mistake, but either a delusion or a very unusual but real experience; and again, if the effect of an unusual experience is to produce a higher degree of effectiveness and rationality, it is the less likely to be a delusion due to some disordering of the mind. Although for instance it is not unusual for a sunstroke to change a sober man into a drunkard, it is very unusual for it to change a Saul into a Paul. Thus in St. Paul's case we have to choose between the alternative of a very unusual experience and a delusion with a very unusual effect.

(b) Secondly, independent coincidence of experiences is a proof of reality. If a number of people under varying circumstances described the appearance of a sea serpent in the same way, it would be very unlikely that it was a mere delusion, and increasingly unlikely with each witness that it was a mistake. But people of all kinds and of all degrees of education describe their spiritual experiences in such a way that they are understood by each other; and differences between races and times pass away under the touch of the same overwhelming experiences. Thus, although it is no doubt the first impulse of a cautious mind to explain an unusual experience as a mistake or a delusion, it is not necessarily the truest impulse.

Now the fact that certain experiences are not universal, may be due to different degrees of perception or of reason. Certain minds are defective in their grasp of some of the ordinary principles of reason, or of perception of mathematical elements, or of moral principles, yet we do not say that perhaps the world is, after all, a chaos, perhaps there is no such thing as an angle, perhaps the deliberate infliction of pain is not to be deprecated. Or it may be that an experience is unusual simply because it implies a higher degree of development than is usually found, or a vital condition of faculties which are apt to decay. Certain distinctions of colour seem to have been unperceived by early races, and are now unperceived by uncivilised races, and the sense of colour and perception of shades is a thing which can be developed even in the individual by exercise. Certain senses too are only at their height during the most robust years of life; it is said that few people after the age of forty can hear the squeak of a bat. Yet in such cases we do not count heads and determine by a majority vote who is right and who is wrong; for even when certain experiences are enjoyed only by a very small fraction of mankind, they are not therefore unreal. Thus the perception of the beauty of a picture by Fra Angelico, or a fugue by Bach, or a drama of Sophocles, is not a universal experience : only a minute proportion of mankind can possibly appreciate these productions; some even are blind, some are deaf and cannot even apprehend, far less appreciate. Yet, the colour, the music, and the words are there, and we believe the beauty and the art to be a reality, not a delusion. So too spiritual experiences may be unusual, because they depend on faculties seldom developed, or on a vital condition of the whole being, but seldom realised.

And lastly, certain facts may be true and may be universally recognisable and yet may be seldom experienced, because the necessary conditions may be difficult of attainment. Few people may be able to describe the opalescent rainbow cloud drifted over the Zambesi Falls, because few people have been to the Zambesi. And it is possible likewise that many of us have no experience of certain spiritual facts, because we do not put ourselves into the conditions under which we could experience them; because we give no time, no thought, or no credit to the subject; and that thus we can keep ourselves apart from spiritual forces unless in God's mercy they burst upon us like a catastrophe.

But if there are coincident experiences asserted by St. Paul and St. Augustine, and by simple, sincere souls in our own day—common to kings and philosophers, to carpenters and fishermen, to Welsh miners of to-day and to mystic souls of the Middle Ages; if there are people in the world who express themselves as being as sure of spiritual realities as of the material things which surround them, those are wilfully blind who do not at least examine these things. For the nature of agnostic and believer alike yearns for some answer to the pressing problems of the world, and there is no other answer that can satisfy the moral nature except to believe that there is a God who sitteth above the water-floods and remaineth a King for ever.

§ 2. The proof of the reality of spiritual experiences does not rest on universal recognition ; for spiritual perception may require special faculties, special development, or special conditions. Only those who acknowledge such experiences could be expected at all to say of what nature the faculty or the conditions must be, and even these may be partly unknown, and the conditions may not be wholly within a man's power. A man may attempt to put himself in the right condition and yet receive no experience, and again, apart from his own effort, the experience may arrive ; just as a man might go to Japan to experience an earthquake and feel no shock, and some night might find his house shaking in a country village in England. Indeed, one of the great conditions which have been indicated by spiritual teachers, is the receptive rather than the active and self-reliant attitude, the open ear, the child-like mind : yet, on the other hand, it is no less strongly asserted that effort and aspiration have their part, and that he who seeks will find.

If the test of reality does not depend on universal recognition, then we have to rest on the word of individuals as to their immediate perceptions ; and absolute conviction will only be produced by our own experience.

But in what way, it may be asked, does such an argument differ from that which has been used to support all kinds of fantastic spiritual theories. Any charlatan may assert, " The proof of my

teaching is my experience ; put yourself under
the conditions I lay down, and you will have
similar experiences ; or if not, it will be shown
that you have not the necessary faculty of
perception."

In form, indeed, our argument does not differ
from any other argument which brings individual
testimony to prove unusual experiences.   All
immediate experience implies right conditions
and right faculties ; and only those who have the
experience can know at all what the conditions
and faculties are.

But the great distinction lies in the place of
these immediate experiences in our whole scheme
of rational belief.   We are not enquiring whether
certain detached experiences can be proved by
the testimony of comparatively few individuals ;
but what we are asking is whether the coincident
experiences of these individuals confirm the conclusion at which we have already arrived on
indirect evidence.

We must therefore ask of what nature spiritual
experiences must be if they are to correspond to
the assumptions of the moral nature ; and whether
the experiences asserted are of this kind.

§ 3. It is obvious that the inner experience must,
in the first place, be an experience of some power.

Our moral consciousness presents us, as we
have seen, with two kinds of facts of apparently
conflicting nature ; on the one hand, the ideals of

perfection and moral obligation ; on the other, the experience of evil.

An elementary philosophic impulse towards unity often leads men to blur this opposition ; to attempt to unify the contradiction by denying that any contrast exists. Thus popular Pantheism obliterates the distinction between good and evil ; or Christian Science tries vainly to assert that evil does not really exist. Such systems do not reconcile the contrast, they merely deny one element of it.[1] No solution can be found in such confusions of thought : there is no harmony of opposing elements except through some power which is more embracing and more real than either of the opposed existences.

The moral demand for completeness makes us seek such a harmonising principle both within

[1] We must notice that the Hegelian conception of God as the *Absolute*, that is, as the sum of all reality, good as well as evil, is not really of the same nature as the Pantheism with which it is often confounded, in which all distinction of good and evil is lost. Thus Mr. Balfour, in discussing the Hegelian theory of the Absolute in the *Foundations of Belief*, p. 155, says : " . . . in its all-inclusive universality it " (*i.e.* the Absolute as identified with God) "holds in suspension, *without preference and without repulsion*," (the italics are mine) "every element alike of the knowable world. Of these none, whatever be its nature, be it good or bad, base or noble, can be considered as alien to the Absolute : all are necessary and all are characteristic."

But this is a total perversion of the Hegelian principle, which is the transcending of immediate being. It would be a false Absolute which excluded preference and repulsion ; as it would, according to Hegel, be a false infinity which excluded time. And the Absolute which contains evil, must contain it *as* evil, that is, as repulsive, to be abhorred, to be contended against, as having no eternal "real" existence ; and in containing good, it must contain it *as* good, that is to say, as preferable, as desirable, and as "real."

and without us; without us, for the moral
demand drives us to look beyond the simple,
sharp contrasts of life in this world to a greater
life beyond, where the injustices of this world will
be righted and its imperfections restored; and
within us, for it impels us to look below our
painful remembrances, our incomplete struggles
after righteousness, to a power which is able to
transform the sin and the sorrow that is past, and
to bring it into a unity of life with the perfect
and the holy for which we yearn and for which
we feel compelled to strive. We need to know
this power therefore as an objective power without us, and as a power working for us; yet our
direct experience of it can only be a power working within us. If then we can have any immediate experience of this power, it must in the
first place be of the nature of inner experience;
experience of some power which is not ourselves
and which is yet within us.

But how would the nature of such experiences
differ from the simple ethical experiences of which
we have already spoken? In our experience of
life we stumble, as it were, across moral facts;
we are confronted by ideas, obligations, imperfect realisations of perfection, which do not, we
recognise, belong to the natural world; they are
facts of another order of things, yet in themselves
they are but incomplete. They must belong to
some system which we cannot wholly see. Now
if we catch a glimpse of this system, if we have a

direct experience of the principle which binds these facts together, will it be like or unlike any which we know?

Let us imagine ourselves crossing over a desert where there are lying great stones of irregular shape and outline which have come down from the cliffs which rise above us: as we stumble among them we suddenly perceive that there are some which seem to show traces of a design and regularities of angle and side. Suddenly the idea strikes us that these stones have something which differentiates them from the rest, something which relates them to each other; we ponder them as they lie, and suddenly before us rises to the mind's eye an edifice, a temple. Is it like the stones? It is like them because they are its constituent parts, but it is unlike them because of its essentially ideal nature. The temple consists of the stones, but it cannot be said to be *like* them, because the temple is the expression of an idea, and the stones in becoming a temple have undergone a transformation, and become part of some great conception of beauty. The power which is able to transform them into a system is a power which itself belongs to some higher region of existence.

Or again if we understand the chemistry of the human body, we know that the conjunction of these chemical elements implies the existence of some power through which they are kept together, some power belonging to a region higher than the region of mere chemistry ; apart from the power which animates them they will change, and dissolution will take place.

Just in the same way our ethical experiences show themselves to us as part of a system ; but the power through which they can become a system is a power of a higher region than the mere ethical experiences themselves.

We name this power according to the highest categories we know. We call it *vital* because life is the greatest transforming power in the objective world ; we call it *spiritual* because this is the greatest power we know within us ; and as regards its quality, we class it with the transforming power of love, which we know in the world of feeling. Love can transform our inner experiences of pain or sorrow, so that they become parts of a greater joy. The very quality of the experience changes, and wrong-doing between man and man can be so blotted out that we call down " blessings on the falling out that all the more endears."

Thus then we apprehend intellectually the nature of the spiritual reality which we require to correspond to our moral nature.

The reality must be a power transcending ethical facts and capable of transforming them. It must be a power within us, or we could not have immediate experience of it, and yet it cannot be our own, for the transformation which our ethical nature demands is the restitution of a universe of things of which we ourselves are only an infinitesimal part.

We shall have to think of this power by help of the greatest conceptions which our minds can reach. If we name it according to the highest categories that we know, we shall call it life, for it works the miracle of life, harmonising opposing elements, transcending lower laws ; but it is a life which belongs to a higher system than any life which we know, and we call it therefore eternal life.

Again we call it love, for in our own individual sphere of action we know that love effects such transformations.

Finally we call it spirit, for spirit is the highest conception under which we can combine the qualities which we have designated. Form, power, righteousness are all abstract terms ; they are powers and qualities of spirit, which is the greatest and most *concrete* [1] reality we know.

[1] Cf. Hegel, *Logic*, *The Doctrine of the Notion*.

B. THE SPIRITUAL REALITIES
—Continued

CHAPTER VI

EVIDENCE OF SPIRITUAL REALITIES

§ 1. So far as we have arrived at an intellectual apprehension of spiritual experiences, it is evident that our definition would exclude the marvels which sometimes have been called spiritual. Supernormal experiences or powers may be accompaniments or signs of spiritual realities, but are not themselves spiritual in any sense which is cogent to our present purpose; for the experience of spiritual reality must be an inner experience of a power which is not ourselves but which is able to transform moral experiences, to conform our will to the moral law, or in other words to sanctify it.

We have next to ask what witness there is to experiences of the kind we have defined; and we are answered by all records of conversion, sudden or gradual, in which the convert becomes conscious at a moment, or through a long period of time, that he is in contact with a spiritual power other than his own.   This evidence is direct.

But it may be said that although we call this evidence direct, our consciousness of the power is only subjective—we know it in ourselves ; and in thinking of it as something other than ourselves we may be misinterpreting a subjective experience.

In admitting this we must admit that the same thing is true about our experience of the presence, of the very existence of a friend.   The external world, the existence of any person in it, is known to us "subjectively"; that they actually exist apart from us is an interpretation, and may be a misinterpretation of our experience, but it is the only rational interpretation of it.   Even so, this interpretation of spiritual experiences might theoretically be a misinterpretation, but is, as we have shown, the practical rational interpretation of our inner ethical experience.

Let us consider then an instance of this consciousness of spiritual power.   In a dissolute age Colonel Gardiner was notorious in his regiment for his profligate life.   When he was alone during some pause in a riotous evening, he sat down to read a book called *The Christian Soldier*, that he might amuse himself with it.   He was aware of a light on his book, and looking up he saw a vision of the Crucified Christ, and with an inner or outer sense he heard the words, "O sinner! did I suffer this for thee, and are these the returns ?"

The horror of sin overwhelmed him, and for some three months, during which he had little hope of salvation, he resolved to spend what was left to him of life in "as rational and as useful a manner as he could." At the end of that time he entered into a rapturous sense of the goodness and mercy of God, in which he lived for seven years, leading a holy and disciplined life in that same regiment in which he had been a byword for his evil living, avoiding, after the manner of his time, a display of "enthusiasm," serving as a gallant and beloved officer, and appearing to those who met him as "so much the Christian, the well-bred man, and the universal friend." The Divine power was consciously experienced by Colonel Gardiner as more real than anything else in his life, for it effected a complete change in its most fundamental realities.[1]

But let us turn to another instance well known to us all—the conversion of St. Paul. Again and again he asserts in the strongest terms this consciousness of a Divine Power—the Spirit of life, the Spirit of Christ, the Spirit of adoption dwelling in us, praying in us, transforming us, so that he can say of himself that he is dead, but that Christ lives in him.

The instances we have given are signal instances of sudden yet permanent conversion, but such instances do not make up the total sum of experiences. Many have felt this consciousness

[1] Doddridge's *Life of Colonel Gardiner.*

of a Divine Presence who have lost it again ; and many, on the other hand, who have had no supreme moment of perception have gradually realised through the course of struggling years, that there was a Power within them, moulding their will in spite of its weakness and infinite imperfections—a Power on which they might rest, through which life and strength flowed into them.

It may be contended that these "spiritual experiences" are merely psychological phenomena subject to psychological laws, and of the same class as psychological phenomena which have obviously nothing to do with religious matters. A change of life is no doubt worked by "repentance and faith," but if we call these qualities in the vernacular "changing your mind," and "expectation," how is the change so worked different from other psychological phenomena, from the conscious change, for instance, of the spendthrift to the miser ?

The fact that spiritual experiences are psychological phenomena and resemble other psychological phenomena has no more bearing on their being spiritual realities than the fact that a reformatory is a physical phenomenon has on the fact of its being also a manifestation of justice. A reality must manifest itself somehow, psychically or physically. From one point of view a reformatory is a material fact of bricks and mortar and so is a public - house, but as a moral phenomenon a reformatory and a public - house have entirely

R

different origins and value and purpose. So the
fact that a man can completely change his mind
is a psychological phenomenon common both to
the spendthrift-turned-miser, and to Saul-become-
Paul, or the drunkard-turned-Christian. But the
question is not whether a man can turn from one
kind of evil-living to another subtler and more
dangerous kind of evil-living—be it miserly or
self-righteous—but whether the whole life of a
man who realises that he is tied and bound with
the chains of sin, can be delivered and renewed
only by the help of some higher life. Those who
experience this change confess the consciousness
of this higher life, and prove by their changed
outlook and altered conduct that the spiritual
reality is effective in the region of the will.

§ 2. The spiritual reality must be psycho-
logically experienced through thought, emotion,
perception. Each of these modes of experience,
but especially the two latter, are liable to be
confused with the spiritual reality itself.

For example, in the book *The Varieties of
Religious Experience* the emotional element in
religious experience is grossly exaggerated at the
expense of the intellectual. This is due to the
unscientific method of the book, in which Professor James has predetermined the element of
emotion as the differentiating element in religious
experience, in striking opposition to the testimony
of mystics and saints. He has consequently

selected those experiences in which the emotional element predominates and the intellectual element is in abeyance, and necessarily comes to the conclusion that the saints are deficient in brains and practical power — a conclusion even ludicrous, when one looks back on the saints of the Jewish Church from the prophets to the Maccabees, and on the saints of the Christian Church from the Apostles to our own day, with the exception of just that specially neurotic class mainly of mediaeval saints whom Professor James has chiefly chosen for study.

It is true that emotion, rising to absolute rapture and falling at times to despair or resting in exquisite peace, is often characteristic of the saintly life, but on these joys the saints themselves have never laid any chief stress, but have warned all those who are attracted by them of the dryness which may follow.

Julian of Norwich for instance describes how after God had shown her "a sovereign ghostly pleasance," she was "turned and left to myself in heaviness and weariness of my life and irksomeness of myself. . . . There was no comfort nor none ease to me but faith, hope, and charity ; and these I had in truth but little in feeling," and she explains that "This Vision was shewed me for that it is speedful to some souls to feel on this wise : sometime to be in comfort, and sometime to fail and to be left to themselves.   And both is one love." [1]

[1] *Revelations of Divine Love*, pp. 34, 35.

This strong consciousness of a personal spiritual power is sometimes accompanied in cases of intense feeling by experiences of another kind apparently in the region of sense. The obvious explanation would be that heightened emotion leads to subjective perception, but that these sense-impressions sometimes precede an emotional or intellectual conversion, like the words heard by Saul, or the vision of the Crucified Christ to Colonel Gardiner.

Without laying stress on such sensational experiences it must be allowed that here too we have among much variation a certain coincidence of experience. As those suffering from alcoholic or from morphia poisoning experience delusions of the same type, even though not precisely similar, so those who are spirit-intoxicated do not see or hear things precisely identical, but things of the same type, lights, harmonies, odours, transfigurations.[1]

> . . . joy that will not cease,
> Pure spaces clothed in living beams,
> Pure lilies of eternal peace,
> Whose odours haunt my dreams.

All these manifestations lead us to conclude that that which is possessing the soul makes it conscious in a high degree of spiritual powers primarily affecting the soul, and thence perhaps communicated to the senses.

Such mystical experiences it may be said are

---

[1] Thus Richard Rolle, an anchorite of the fourteenth century, distinguishes three stages in contemplation—Warmth, Sweetness, and Melody.

the symptoms of a diseased mind.   But the stir-
ring of the senses is not in itself a disease.   We
know that the sense apparitions of morphia or
alcohol are diseased, because we know from other
proofs that body and mind are deteriorating ; and
that though the delusions are not direct perceptions of evil powers they are the direct results of
evil powers.   But if the mind of a visionary is
otherwise strong and wise as is frequently the
case, and if the sensational experiences are the
accompaniment of a character which is growing
in strength and sincerity and sweetness, then we
have no more reason to call the mind of a mystic
diseased than the mind of an artist, who experiences raptures which other men do not know.

The mystics themselves do not lay great stress
on sensational experiences, which even in a decep-
tive sweetness may be the work of the devil
instead of the work of God ; nor on emotional
experiences, which, however exquisite, are gifts
which for the soul's own health may be denied ;
nor even on intellectual apprehension though God
gives wisdom liberally, but what they do lay stress
on is the attitude of the will, and the mystic
union with the Divine which is as real, and sometimes even more vital in times of " dryness " than
in joy.

§ 3. How then do these considerations affect the
question of what the mind really apprehends under
all or any of these forces ?   The believer holds

that he is in contact with a spirit mightier than his own—with a Divine Spirit. The sceptic retorts that this conclusion cannot be reached on reasonable grounds. It is true that this conclusion cannot be demonstratively proved like a fact within the scope of what we call exact knowledge. But what are truly "reasonable grounds" when our most certain conclusion is the limitation of our knowledge? How if our philosophy leads us to believe that we have only touched the lower notes of a scale whose completion our ears are too dull to hear; that we are standing on the "altar stairs that slope through darkness up to God"? How if all our knowledge and all our philosophy bring us to believe that what we know most truly, we know but as the beginning of things which lead us every way beyond our reach?

For we are not living in a finite world at all; everything we touch is really the centre of an infinite world although our knowledge of it is limited. The finiteness is in our knowledge and the forces under which we perceive existence, not in that which exists.

> Flower in the crannied wall,
> I pluck you out of the crannies—
> Hold you here, root and all, in my hand,
> Little flower—but if I could understand
> What you are, root and all, and all in all,
> I should know what God and man is.

If we started at the heart of one small plantain that we pull up on the lawn, and thoroughly understood the relation and proportion, the chemical properties, the laws of cohesion and gravitation, the colour, the growth, the life that is in it and its relation to the universe, we should feel the small star of green leaves leading us to the knowledge of stars and suns, back through the history of the past, on to the future, down to the heart of life.   We could not understand what it is, and how it has come to be and continues in being, without knowing the laws that govern all things, and being brought back to the power that makes the world.

If we start thus at any centre in the material world we are led on to the conception of Infinite Power ; but if we take into account not only a part of the world, that part which we call external and material, but the whole world, the universe of existence, including the inner world with its moral and spiritual experiences, we are led on to see that this Infinite Power must be also a Spiritual Power.

§ 4. Now, from whatever portion of experience, inner or outer, our consideration begins, we find one thing always bound up with it—that is, Personality.   We start from our own personality, the " I " which feels that which comes through the senses; the " I " which thinks that which comes through the senses ; which is the unity of all experience to us, by virtue of which alone we know that the world exists.   Yet when we come to examine this " I," to think of this personality which is the ground of all our assurance, it is perhaps its limits which most puzzle us. In an abnormal case such as that of Mr. Hanna, it is possible, as we see, to have two distinct chains of memory and experience characterised by different qualities, both claiming recognition and exclusive recognition, yet the one will was able to accept both or reject either.

This is an extreme case, but we all know the same phenomenon more or less; we can all look back on some part of our life which we remember as if it were a tale of some one else, thought out or read of by ourselves; we all have to believe in previous years of which we have not even a memory, but which those who know us identify as indeed our own; we all in later life look on certain regions of feeling, fierce desires of our youth, as parts of ourselves entranced or dead; we all nightly have to suffer or enjoy experiences whose vividness has in the day faded into a mere fancy soon forgotten, or a lapse during which the world, whose existence to us depends on our consciousness, has moved on with steady pace. Our minds which tell us that the very existence of the universe means nothing without consciousness, yet point us back to a time before our own or any human consciousness existed, and on to an unknown in front of us beyond the river of death.

We are conscious, too, of workings in the soul which do not seem to originate in itself; of a longing inwards or outwards beyond the personality we

know, and of a response ; of more definite questionings and of a clearer reply ; of a Power which
does not seem our own aiding our weaker wills ;
of life lived in relation to the Unseen ; of as clear
a conviction of the worthlessness of all existence
without a Spirit in the universe, as of the chaos
and nothingness of a world without Reason.

We cannot believe in the world without an
interpenetrating Reason ; no more can we understand mind unless we assume the existence of
a Mind beyond human minds.   It is not our
requirements only, but our experience which force
on us this conviction.

The change from the older philosophy to the
newer has been compared to the Copernican
revolution in astronomy.   Instead of taking the
earth as the centre round which sun and moon
and planets moved, the centre of the system of
which we are a part was assumed to be the sun,
and movements which had been incomprehensible were understood.   So the older Greek philosophers began with the study of the world, and
worked inward to the study of the mind of man.
The great revolution in thought achieved by Kant
was to reverse the process, and to examine the
content of experience through which alone we
know that there is a world at all.

Now we know that our solar system is only
one of many, and is rushing with incredible swift-
ness through the vasts of space, whither we cannot
tell.   That it is so moving explains to us many

appearances which otherwise we could not understand, and it may be that some time the vast distant centre shall swim into sight, and that all things uncomprehended in the universe of stars will be clear to us.

So too we find that the examination of experience, the study of the mind of man, leaves much unexplained.   There is much that we cannot understand, of which we can only say that it must depend on some vast power beyond.   It cannot be less than the powers we know but infinitely greater ; it cannot understand less of righteousness, nor feel less of love, nor be less active in the creation of ideals, nor possess less formative power than these ideals ; it cannot be less than personal then, it must be infinitely more.   The least that it can be is a Spirit for whom the world is, as well as through whom it is ; for whom we are before we exist for ourselves ; for whom all exists before it has begun to be and when the manner of its present existence has ceased ; a Power of whom and through whom and unto whom are all things.

PART IV

THE MYSTERY OF PERSONALITY

A. VERIFICATION OF PRINCIPLES
IMPLIED IN HIGHER EXPERIENCE

CHAPTER I

§ 1. THERE is then a natural world and an ideal world; a world as it appears in time, and a world of that which ought to be which is perpetually realising itself.

The natural world comprises all physical things and all the responses which these things cannot but make to one another, from the response of particle to particle which we call gravitation, up to the response of the nerves to the pleasure of an evening landscape or the sound of a voice singing. But man, and possibly the higher animals also, have come within view of the wider horizon, the world of what ought to be, of things claiming a response which it is yet possible to refuse; a world in which choice, will, and purpose are determining causes.

It is only through the development of mind that this ideal ever is developed, that the ideal world begins, so far as we know, to exist in experience. But having once come within the sphere of experience it claims universal empire; there is a perpetual strife, a continual invasion, which cannot cease until that which is, is made as it ought to be; and not even then will the intellectual ideal be satisfied until it is shown that what has been was already in its time and place what it ought to have been.

In three great degrees the chasm between the natural and ideal world is bridged.

(*a*) The external world is only known to man in terms of mind; the material of science is experience, and experience is impossible without the formative principle of perception and thought through which our many sensations become to us a world of objects. Man has set his mark on the world even through the fact of knowing it; he can only know it through its becoming his own, and he could not know it as a reasonable system unless there was a reason in it corresponding to that reason through which he knows it.

(*b*) But every action of man in the world is the action of an idea: through the action of ideals the primitive world becomes the civilised world, and these ideals write their record in history.

(*c*) And finally, the power of faith, springing to the conception of an answering wisdom in the universe, becomes an effective power. Just as man's reason assumes an answering reason in-

finitely greater, so the soul of man, shaping out
purposes, working towards ends, and in its own
measure originating, must assume the counterpart
of his soul in the universe—a soul of the universe
on an infinite scale, working towards ends, shaping
purposes according to laws of righteousness, perfection, and love. Through faith in this wisdom
man rises into a region in which he can gain a
more immediate knowledge of that which he
reasons must exist, a Presence transcendent yet
immanent in the world. He comes into a spiritual
region in which his experiences though individual
are not isolated ; he finds that that experience
which is most intimate to him is also common
to others ; and therefore, as his own experience
widens, he learns also to recognise that others
may have had fuller and deeper experience of the
same kind, and to trust in this region as in others,
authority and guidance from outside, as well as to
his own growing perception.

Yet he must face the possibility that a wrong
interpretation of a real experience may be given by
himself and others—that he may be misinterpreting subjective movements of his own spirit when
he believes himself in contact with a spiritual power
other than his own. We have shown how the
verification of the belief in our interpretation rests
in the first place upon its rationality, its correspondence to the demands of our moral nature,
but is there also any objective standard to which
we can appeal ?

Let us turn back again to the question of historical revelation. We have seen that historical facts cannot prove the truth of a revelation if they are considered alone and out of relation to spiritual experience. But the moral claims and the spiritual experience of man point in one direction ; let us then examine the historical revelation in relation to these claims and this experience, and see how far it will afford a verification of their reality and the interpretation which we cannot but put on them.

§ 2. By a rough analogy we may compare this method of verification which we are now about to follow, with that by which the planet Neptune was discovered. Certain astronomical movements had been observed which could not be ascribed to the effect of any heavenly bodies then known ; but it was calculated that the movements and deflections noticed would be accounted for if, in a particular direction, a planet hitherto unperceived existed. The telescope was turned in this direction, and in the depths of night and space Neptune came into sight.

So from the experiences of life and the world we have drawn various conclusions ; we have said that if certain facts are to be reconciled at all or regarded as part of a great world system, the explanation and completion of them must lie in a certain direction. Our inner experience corresponds with these conclusions, but we look outwards also for some objective realisation of the spiritual idea ; and as we turn our telescope upon the world's history, a star comes into view.

At a definite time in the world's history Christianity came into existence, not as a religious philosophy, but as a series of events, manifested in a Personality[1] and developed in a life history, the significance of which was only afterwards realised by those who had taken part in these events.

But it may be objected that such a verification has no real value, and cannot ever give confirmation to the results already arrived at; that the process is in no sense comparable to the method of Neptune's discovery, for there reasoning led to a certain conclusion, and direct observation confirmed it. Here our reasoning leads perhaps to some general conclusions, but not with at all the same certainty as in mathematical reasoning ; and instead of turning for confirmation to the evidence of the senses we are only directed to another similar theory put forth with more or less definiteness at a certain period in history. The "verification" would lie not simply in the fact that Christ lived and died, but that He lived the Incarnate Word and died as a ransom for many ; this is "the significance of events," and it is no historic fact, but a philosophy which originated in the yearning of the human soul for redemption. This philosophy no doubt professes to be a

[1] Expressed in the phrase "the Word became flesh."

S

revelation from God, but what is revelation? We have to judge on the ground of its content whether it is true, that is, whether it is really a revelation.

It is true that between the verification suggested and the astronomical verification there is only an analogy; an illustration from one sphere of knowledge can only apply incompletely to another sphere. But the use of the astronomical analogy is to draw attention to this particular fact that the process described is not, as the objection assumes, a purely subjective process, a philosophy simply fitted on to historical events.

Revelation in its larger sense is the other side of discovery. Man speaks of himself as discovering that which is being revealed, whether by God or by Nature. The process of revelation does not dispense with discovery but implies it. All truth always exists; it is revealed bit by bit only, because man can only discover it bit by bit. When we speak of sudden revelation or of Divine revelation we mean some increase of the normal powers of man by which he is able to take in truth in a speedier or larger way than by the ordinary application of normal human faculties. We do not mean that there is any change in truth itself.

But an eternal truth may manifest itself in time. The truths of Nature are in a sense eternal, the laws of animal life for instance are always true, but, so far as we know, there was

a time when animal life did not exist, and there
may be such a time to come : thus the eternal
truths of life have an actual or historical manifestation.

But revelation by means of historical manifestation does not dispense with the process of
discovery ; the truth of the historical manifestation
is open only to those who can comprehend it,
just as eternal truths of Nature though historically
manifested, must be observed in their manifestation and their significance must be discovered.
The significance of the historical truth must imprint
itself on the individual experience. Yet although
the truth of a revelation in history may have to
be tested and discovered by human faculties, it is
not therefore wholly subjective, wholly developed
out of the human reason : it is not what we call a
" mere theory."

Christianity is essentially distinguished from
religious philosophy in that it is not only the
revelation of a system, but of a personality and of
a history. Let us then examine three of the
greatest and most essential doctrines of that
revelation, briefly as is necessary, and see how
these compare with the demands and spiritual
principles which we have already arrived at. Three
such great doctrines are those of the Fatherhood
of God, of the Sacrifice of Christ, and of the Spirit
in the Church.

The question will again instantly arise as to
how it is possible for a personality or a history to

confirm a philosophical theory; and those who tend to separate Christian ethics from the personality of Christ, and Christian doctrines from the consideration of the human life and character of Christ and Christians, will be prepared to dispute the possibility. It is argued, for example, that the teaching of Christ about the Fatherhood of God is not essentially connected with the doctrine of His own personality; the belief in the Fatherhood of God, it might be said, is a belief which is common to all races of man and evolved in the course of human history; that Christ taught it needs no special confirmation, and is at any rate in no way connected with the question of His own divine sonship.

Again, it might be said that the idea of the sacrifice of Christ consummated by His death is a doctrine evolved from primitive superstition, refined into a spiritual and possibly true religious theory, and fitted on to a peculiarly commanding and attractive personality, but not essentially connected with this personality or with this human history.

Finally, the communion in the mystical body of Christ, the body inspired by the Spirit of God, is, it may be argued, a poetical imagination based on metaphor rather than reasoning, and applied to the organisation which formed itself after Christ's death; but this doctrine again is not essentially connected with the personality of Christ nor with the history of the body of believers.

We have already tried to deal with some of these arguments from the defensive point of view, and to show, for example, that the evolution of an idea only concerns the method of its growth, not the content of the idea nor the question of its truth.

What remains therefore is to treat these questions from the positive side, and this we shall have to do from the Christian point of view, and in terms of the usual Christian phraseology.

We shall then try to show what this phraseology implies in terms of our ordinary life, and to see thereby the connection of the doctrines so expressed with human experience, to find in fact what constitutes their *reality* for us.

We shall attempt to show how these doctrines are, from the Christian point of view, connected with the personality of Christ, connected, that is, with a historic reality.

And we must then leave any one who has followed so far, to judge for himself if this historic "revelation" both fulfils those demands of the human mind and spirit and confirms the objective interpretation of spiritual experience.

§ 3. An attempt, as we have said, is frequently made in our own time to separate Christian ethics from Christian doctrine.   Many of those who call themselves Christians and of those who profess themselves agnostics make this separation ; the latter generally allow that the ethical teaching of

Christ is the highest and most spiritual teaching ever given, and the former boast that what Christianity really means to them is uprightness and honesty and living at peace with one's neighbour.

The inadequacy of this view of life which thus separates ethics from metaphysics is evident even from the naturalistic standpoint. Any one who, through a study of science or history, has become aware of the greatness of the world in its present existence, its past and its future, must at once realise that though the conception of duty is one of the highest and most spiritual things in the world, it is only one part even of the heritage of humanity, and bears a still smaller proportion to the richness of the whole universe. It is the neglect of this perception of proportion which often proves a stumbling-block to those in whom the love of beauty amounts to a passion. To such it must seem that the worshippers of duty, living in a world of light and freedom, have made a cramped prison for their souls; and the conclusion of beauty-loving souls that if this is what religion means they will have none of it, is from this point of view not only excusable but justifiable.

But if the inadequacy of this theory is evident from the naturalistic point of view, it is far more evident from the religious point of view. For in any religion the centre of existence must lie altogether beyond the limits of this world, and man is no longer, as to the intelligent agnostic, the climax of existence.   On the contrary his relation to all things that exist must be conditioned by his relation to God as the origin and ground of all things.

B. EXAMINATION OF THREE FUNDA- MENTAL CHRISTIAN DOCTRINES

CHAPTER II

THE FATHERHOOD OF GOD

§ 1. The idea of the Fatherhood of God has perhaps not been absent even from some of the most primitive religions; and even polytheistic religions embody in the name of their supreme deity the idea of fatherhood. The metaphor of fatherhood was one among many of the metaphors used to express the relation of God to Israel.

But from Christ and His followers the idea of fatherhood received a fuller and deeper signi- ficance; it was used to express a higher and yet a more intimate relation, through the belief that man, originally made in God's image but sepa- rated from God by sin, could by a "new birth" become a child of God in a fuller sense.

The Christian doctrine of the fatherhood of God thus involves the belief that the origin and source of existence, although a Spirit, is not qualified like our spirits by the limitations of

individual existence. The source of sin lies in
the separation of the individual from God, and
Christianity therefore finds the reconciliation
with God in the imparting of Divine life. The
Christian doctrine of the fatherhood of God
thus involves many beliefs which we have already
touched upon.

The broad basis on which it rests is the
belief in God as the creator and sustainer of all
things, and is thus in complete opposition not
only to the materialist view of the world, but to
all philosophies, dualistic or idealistic, which identify
matter with the element of evil in the world, or
attempt to reduce it to a simple unreality.

Yet if we look at the teaching of Christ and
His apostles we may be struck at first by the fact
that although there are passages clearly affirming
the providence of God in relation to the lower
creatures, the redemption of the whole creation
and the final restitution of all things, yet there is
comparatively little about the world apart from
man. But what does the world apart from man
mean to us now, compared with what it meant
then? While our interest in the material creation
has increased, our interest in spiritual beings
other than man has lessened. We are less sure
of their existence, and in consequence the importance of the question does not greatly appeal
to us, and thus we tend to leave out of sight the
great part of Christianity which is occupied with
the spiritual world.

But if we look more broadly at the whole of Christian teaching, and more especially if we consider it in historical relation to the beliefs of the time, we see that Christianity makes the supreme value of the human spirit more manifest by considering it in connection with the whole divine creation as then conceived, spiritual as well as material. Thus the providence of God, not only in every detail of human life, but over every captive bird, is made more forcible when these are considered as parts of a world which includes not only stars and suns, forces of Nature, organic and inorganic existences, but thrones, dominations, and powers.

The idea of Divine Providence, the consciousness of a Personal Mind directing the course of the world and of our lives, is one of the simplest and the strongest appeals made by any religious theory. Many who have not become conscious of a need to be liberated from sin have a strong yearning for the knowledge of a fatherly providence over their lives, and believe that they have a direct experience of it; the consciousness of such a providence grows with growing experience. The child finds that gradually as he lives his ordinary life, without knowledge or will of his own, his whole stature, his physical and emotional nature, his mind itself, is changing. If he is thoughtful he begins to realise that there is a force within him which he does not fully know and can only partially control, shaping his very self, moulding even his thought.

So too at a later age, when the attention is turned upon the experience of life, when the man sees the results of limitations which at the time seemed only to cramp the powers ; of troubles that seemed irremediable ; of apparently chance events which yet changed the whole current of life— then even those who have not hitherto accepted any belief in a spiritual force in the world often become suddenly aware that by means of all these things their lives have been shaped with a wisdom they were slow to realise, and a love in which they dared not hope, and recognise that

> There's a divinity that shapes our ends.

Far more then do those whose wills have been set to carry out the will of God and to look for His providence and His love, find a confirmation of their belief when they see how through sickness and health, through loneliness as well as through the mutual offices of friendship, a Father has been leading them, strengthening, chastising, and comforting.

§ 2. But the belief in the fatherhood of God implies more than the belief in Him as the origin of all things ; a deeper conception is implied in His relation to men who can know Him and obey Him as a son obeys his father. The idea of the fatherhood of God was more developed among the Jews than among other nations of ancient

times.   Historically, the earliest conception was
that of the sonship of Israel as a nation, and the
highest vision of the prophets rose to the idea of
God as the Father, not of Israel only, but of
other nations.   But the fatherhood of God in
the Christian sense includes much more than the
belief in the relation of God to any race of men,
or to mankind as a whole, namely, the relation
between God and the individual soul.

The idea of a conscious moral relation to God
involves, as we have said, more than the belief
in God as the source of life; for the conscious
moral relation brings us at once face to face with
the element of evil in the world, and demands
a full recognition of it.   Whether or no we hold
that Christ was merely using the language of
the time in speaking of demoniac possession, there
is no doubt that His teaching and that of His
disciples implied the existence of a spirit of evil
so potent as to be sometimes irresistible by
man without the special grace of God—able to
harass not only the human spirit but the human
body and free to have his time or "hour"; yet
a foe of power not limitless, whose very injuries
could be used to work out the purposes of God,
so that the "messenger of Satan" to trouble the
body could be at the same time the executor of
God's curative punishment to the soul.

There is no doubt that Christ and the Apostles
took this view of the power and nature of evil.
How does it correspond to our human experience?

Do we find as life goes on that evil is more or less of a real power in the world and in ourselves? As we look abroad in the world at the evil around us—at nations in convulsion, at the degradation of the innocent, the strength of evil men, the sorrows of those who know not their right hand from their left, the sufferings of Nature—are we more or less conscious of the reality and power of evil? As we aspire to do better do we become more or less conscious of a spiritual power which either opposes our better will or compasses us with ingenious deceptions?

Yet this consciousness of the power of evil is not a consciousness of the dominance of evil; on the contrary, the belief in the reality of evil as a power not ourselves, gives us a greater strength and freedom to oppose it than the paralysing belief that the totality of evil we are conscious of is all inherently our own.

Here again the theory of Christianity, in opposition to pessimistic philosophies whether Agnostic or Calvinistic, expresses the universal human experience of the power of evil and the ineradicable human hope.

Further, the Christian theory assumes the freedom but not the unqualified freedom, of the will. It implies in phrases that speak of the inheritance of the sin of Adam the fact known as well to ordinary experience as to science, that no individual begins the world wholly without moral inheritance; through inheritance as well as

through the early influence of circumstance and
example, tendencies both bad and good are
ingrained in a child, and by the time he has come
to the full use of reason, faults and virtues have
begun to develop.   Thus the will is not free in
the sense that it is unqualified by good and evil
desires.

Yet although the Christian theory recognises
as fully as the determinist theory the inheritance
of tendencies and the force of circumstances, it
preserves the other element of human experience
which the determinist eradicates from his theory
but cannot root out of his mind—that is, the
consciousness of a power of choice.

And again, the philosophy of Christianity
recognises the limited power of the individual
to carry out even that which he sets himself to
do.   It is St. Paul's personal experience of insufficient power to carry out that which his
mind assures him is good and his will assents to,
that drives him to cry out, "O wretched man
that I am, who shall deliver me from the body of
this death?"   And he finds his only answer in
his belief in a power which can not only inspire
the mind but empower the will, and this he calls
God's grace.   Through God's grace, according
to the Christian theory, the human spirit which
through the morbid taint of evil had begun to
die, can be regenerated ; so that man the creature
of God can become the child of God, born again
"not of corruptible seed but of incorruptible,"

through the word of God. This is the Christian philosophy of the birth of the Spirit or, according to a forensic rather than a vital metaphor, "the adoption of sons."

§ 3. Such is the teaching of Christianity on the subject of the Fatherhood of God : but if we take the Christian teaching alone, apart from the personality of Christ, we shall find ourselves merely comparing the religious philosophy of two thousand years ago with the religious philosophy of our own day. The appeal to history would mean no more than this.

But Christianity is essentially more than a theory ; it is the revelation of a life among men. In no case can we understand the full meaning of any teaching if we separate the doctrine from the teacher ; least of all can we hope for a full understanding of Christianity apart from Christ. We cannot judge Christ's teaching apart from His life, nor His life apart from His character, nor any of these apart from His personality. The critic who can give us least assurance that we have before us the very sayings of Christ must all the more attribute the power of Christianity to the effect of the personality of Christ upon His contemporaries.[1]

---

[1] The direct historical justification for attributing the power of Christianity to the personality of Christ rather than to His ethical teaching is found in most early Christian writers, notably in St. Paul, who quotes little of Christ's ethical teaching, but whose Christian ethics sprang from the consciousness of Christ's life in himself and in the whole Christian body.

There is no doubt that Christ taught the fatherhood of God with a fulness and depth with which no one else had taught it, and we cannot separate the teaching from the character of the teacher. " Which of you convinceth me of sin ? " is a question which has never yet been answered. We cannot separate the teaching of the fatherhood of God from the life of perfect sonship. We have to remember that the same lips which spoke the teaching, prayed, " Father, not my will, but thine be done," and in the last agonies of crucifixion breathed out life with words of commendation to His Father's hands.

And we cannot separate life, teaching, and character from personality. "No one knoweth . . . the Father save the Son and he to whomsoever the Son willeth to reveal him." If He who was thus revealing the Father to mankind was not the Son, who was He? And how could He be in life and character what He was ?

It was after the high hopes which had attended the earlier years of His mission had fallen to the ground, after death seemed to have ended all, that events occurred which suddenly illuminated in the minds of His disciples the effect which His life and character and teaching had been all the time producing. It was then only that they could understand what He meant by "my Father and your Father, my God and your God," then only that they could rejoice that He went away and understand that it was expedient for them, since only through death could the promise of the Father come to them, the Spirit of Christ be shed abroad in their hearts, leading them into all truth, saying to them the things which He could not say before, since they were not prepared to receive them.

It was only this return, this rebirth within them, which could fully illuminate for them the mystery of His personality.

T

B. EXAMINATION OF THREE FUNDA-MENTAL CHRISTIAN DOCTRINES
—Continued

CHAPTER III

THE REDEMPTION THROUGH THE SON

§ 1. BEFORE we go on to examine the second of the essential ideas we have indicated, we must, however, note one special difficulty of the subject. In religion perhaps above all things, confusion may be caused by the use of metaphorical language. All language of course is symbolical, words are nothing else but symbols to express thoughts and things ; and language is developed through the metaphorical transference of words, originally symbols of some object or idea, to other objects or ideas. When we talk of *unity* for instance, we use an abstract mathematical symbol to designate a real, vital condition ; when we speak of the *stability of a State* we use terms drawn from material images to designate a social condition. This process of transference is always going on, so that the meaning of words is seldom absolutely definite; we are often aware in the course of argument of the ambiguities to which such transference of language leads; and we can usually guard against these ambiguities by explanations, definitions, and designation of the objects and ideas to which they are applied. But in religion such safeguarding is difficult, continual definition is hardly possible, and a solemn definition is an historic event, for it signifies a crisis of thought which cannot be often repeated; so that the words used in the definition itself have time to change their meaning before another is made; they become less adequate to their purpose or less accurate. We can seldom avoid ambiguity by designating the idea or the object we mean; and the errors that thus creep into any statement of doctrine are multiplied by the process of deductive reasoning.

For instance, when we attempt to qualify our conception of the Divine by the words "Unity" or "Trinity," we are applying abstract mathematical terms to a conception of infinite reality. When we speak of the fatherhood of God we are applying the metaphor of the most vital relation we know, though only a human and finite relation, to the relation between the Infinite and the finite: when we argue from such a relationship we are arguing from a premise which is necessarily inadequate, and if we treat the premise as accurate or complete, our deductions must necessarily become more and more untrue.

But terms are relative too, not only to the contemporary thought on the special subject, but also to the general conceptions of the time; terms of theological definition are chosen from the legal, the scientific, the philosophical phraseology of the period; and not only do the theological conceptions develop and change, but with the development of science and philosophy the meaning of this phraseology, which has been drawn from them, itself alters, or a new development of thought suggests more appropriate phraseology. St. Paul often expressed himself in terms of juridic law where we should express ourselves in terms of natural law, and his forensic language often seems forced to us; so that if we concentrate attention on the imagery, not on the spirit of his argument, his theological expressions seem to belong to a sphere apart from human life and thought. Thus not only does the applicability of a metaphor alter as we know more about the subject to which it is applied, but it alters also as we know more about the region of things from which the metaphor is drawn, or as new regions of knowledge come into view. For new metaphors suggest themselves as more applicable, the meaning of the old metaphors changes, the content of the very words alters, and the expansion of religious thought is checked if truth is identified with one method of expression.

§ 2. The difficulties caused by ambiguity of

language are not greater in any region of religion than in that which concerns the Christian theory of sacrifice. The ideas of sacrifice and propitiation reach back through the whole history of man into barbaric times, if not into times of primitive savagery, and with the moral and intellectual development of man and the evolution of his religious beliefs the content of these ideas has been continually changing; for this idea of the relation of God to man, the idea of what by a human metaphor was called God's "wrath," the idea of God Himself during the ages has been changed, expanded, and purified.

While the idea of sacrifice in religion thus has a long historical development, our growing knowledge of Nature seems to show with continually greater completeness the absolute necessity of sacrifice in the natural world; and the inner moral experience of the individual man continually testifies to the necessity for sacrifice if he would have any true vital relation with God or with his fellow-men.

But what is the connection, it may be asked, between the idea of sacrifice in religion, in the natural world, and in the social world. If monotheism means anything it means a unity of the natural and spiritual world, and it is only because of this fundamental unity that any symbol or symbolic language can be true of spiritual ideas; it is because of this unity that natural religion is in part the discovering of God, for God reveals

Himself through His natural order, and men arrive, for instance, at the idea of the renewal of life by consideration of the rising and setting of the sun, the burial of winter and the resurrection of spring, the generation and regeneration of things. Man belongs to Nature and to Spirit, and his nature and his spirit are not wholly distinct : thus the necessities for sacrifice in the natural world run on and develop into the spiritual principle of sacrifice.

In Nature sacrifice is necessitated : Nature must sacrifice the sprouting impulses of the fifty seeds to the full strength and blossom of the one. In the lower animal creation sacrifice is what we call "instinctive," as when the mother bird exposes herself to danger to protect her young ; in the higher creatures sacrifice is a more or less deliberate act ; and among human beings sacrifice, while it does not cease to be partly necessitated and partly instinctive, becomes still more conscious and even completely voluntary. At this point we speak of it as self-sacrifice.

Thus as there is a development of the ceremonial expression of religious sacrifice, so there is a development of sacrifice in life, from the purely necessitated sacrifice to the completely voluntary sacrifice. It must be noticed that most sacrifices are what is technically called "vicarious," that is, they are sacrifices of one or more individuals for the sake of others. The only sacrifices which are not at least in part *vicarious* are either the

sacrifices of worldly prudence—that is, the sacrifice of some self-interest for the sake of another
self-interest, or the religious sacrifices which are
made simply for the glory of God without consideration of the religious community.[1]

The development of sacrifice in Nature and life,
and the development of sacrifice as a religious
observance, are of course fundamentally connected, for religious observances are the material
expression of conceptions formed from or illuminated by experience.

Whatever view we take of the origin of sacrifice as a religious observance—whether we believe
it to arise from a natural impulse to give gifts or
tribute in order to please a Power above man, or
from the belief in a bond of communion between
a tribe and its totem-god ; or from the supposed
necessity of feeding the spirits of ancestors—whatever alternative is chosen, we must regard the
religious observance as being the expression of
the relationship supposed to exist between living
man and other beings.[2] If ancestor worship is the
primal type, the relation of men to their ancestors
suggests the act which is ritualised ; in another
case the ritual of the blood-covenant and the
relationship it establishes lies at the basis of sacrifice ; or again on the third supposition, if a gift is

[1] Sacrifices for the glory of God generally include either some element
of spiritual prudence or of vicarious sacrifice for others.

[2] If the origin of sacrifice is in sympathetic magic it is not yet a religious
observance ; it only begins to be religious when it is connected with some
spirit or deity.

known to render the human power propitious, it is supposed to be operative in the same way between God and man, or is simply offered as a thanksgiving. But whatever is the origin of sacrifice it is plain that as religious observance it is not wholly distinct from the social relationships which develop on a basis of natural necessities and moral relations.

It would be then unreal to stereotype the idea of religious sacrifice at any one period of its development, to treat as literal the terms in which it was then expressed, and to argue from these terms as from an adequate definition.

It is such reasoning which has made many religious-minded people at the present time misunderstand and repudiate the whole theory of vicarious sacrifice. It is true that such people do not really examine the history or the meaning of the idea when they condemn by some such phrase as "propitiatory machinery" a conception which is essentially vital.

The Christian theory of sacrifice has been very generally identified, and therefore often rejected, with an extreme Calvinistic theory founded on some uses of the word "propitiation." The word propitiate is there used in such senses as to propitiate or blot out the sin, and to propitiate or appease God. In this latter sense is implied the idea of the wrath of God against sin, which under an anthropomorphic image sums up one of the great principles of Christianity, a principle of fundamental optimism. For the fundamental hope of Christianity is in a Power which is greater than the power of evil in the world, and which is in continual opposition to it ; so that iniquity, oppression, and all forms of evil indulgence are penalised, and the evil doer cannot go unscathed.

Yet the anthropomorphic image implies also that the source from which these penalties proceed is not regarded as a blind fate, an impersonal law, but a Personal Will. The very conception of God's justice as an "emotion" implies that the victorious power of good is no mechanical law but a spiritual or personal existence.

Thus at the root of the idea of propitiation, or the possibility of "turning away the wrath of God," lie the great fundamental conceptions of the recognition of sin, the victorious power of righteousness, the personality of this power, and the possibility of forgiveness.

These conceptions are not mere theories but experiences to those who hold them, and believe themselves to have observed as an actual fact that though sin produces its evil fruit to the third and fourth generation, yet the recovery of the sinner is possible.

When however this best and hopeful conception is expressed in the anthropomorphic language of a stern and unchristian age, and garnished with almost savage imagery, when these terms and images are taken as an adequate definition of

facts from which a system can be deductively constructed, we get some such monstrous scheme of
Calvinism as that popularised by Milton, implying
an angry God demanding to be appeased for
some outrage viewed as personal, rejoicing in the
shedding of blood, and esteeming the suffering of
the innocent the only adequate satisfaction for the
sin of the guilty. So conceived, Christianity
would imply not that God so loved the world, but
that God so hated the world that His Son had
to appease Him by the offering of Himself.

From such a scheme every Christian mind
must revolt, and it is difficult to understand
why such a theory should be regarded by any
intelligent person as an expression of Christian
doctrine.

§ 3. If we wish to arrive at the Christian idea
of sacrifice we must put together the principles
found in the recorded teaching of Christ on the
subject of sacrifice. Nothing is clearer in Christ's
teaching than His insistence on the necessity for
sacrifice ; for example in the stern saying, " If
any man come to me, and hate not his father and
mother, yea, and his own life also, he cannot be
my disciple " ; but equally strong is His teaching
of the ultimate bliss of sacrifice drawn from the
same image of the closest and holiest affections—
" There is no man that hath left mother or father
or children or lands . . . but he shall receive a
hundredfold now in this time and in the world to

come eternal life"; or speaking of the same supreme sacrifice of life, "Whosoever shall lose his life for my sake and the gospel's the same shall save it." The sacrifice of life is the ultimate term of sacrifice, and the final result of it is the passing through death to the heart of life itself.

Again, the unity of principle between the natural world and the unseen realities of the spiritual world is shown in the parable, "Except a corn of wheat fall into the ground and die, it abideth alone: but if it die it bringeth forth much fruit."

In the Synoptic Gospels little is recorded of Christ's teaching on the subject of His own sacrifice, but that little is absolutely clear and decisive. "The Son of Man came not to be ministered unto, but to minister, and to give his life a ransom for many," and "This is my body which is given for you . . . my blood which is shed for you and for many for the remission of sins."

What realities in life, in the world, in history, illustrate for us the meaning of such sayings? Are they merely to be received by those who accept them as mystic utterances descriptive of some incomprehensible ideas which we are to receive as facts and act upon as if they were a charm ; or are they statements of a universal truth containing indeed more than our limited knowledge allows us fully to understand, but so bound up with our knowledge of the world and our experience of life that they can be partially realised even by those who do not accept the Christian statement?

This is the question which we must attempt to answer in the next few pages.

What is it which necessitates sacrifice at all? In the earliest stages of life sacrifice appears to be the result of limitation; the struggle for existence among plants must go on because there are too many claimants for one plot of ground. Among animals and men the struggle becomes a more conscious competition in which the weakest is worsted. But here a new principle comes in: the weakest would always fall if it were not for a principle of unity which in its highest stages is the law of love. This principle forms the bond that holds together families, tribes, and states of animals and men, and involves the frequent and even voluntary sacrifice of the strong for the protection of the weak.

Thus sacrifice is necessitated by life and by limitation; by the bond of unity and by the force of opposition; in the supremest type it is necessitated by love and by sin.

Whether the sacrifice of Christ is considered as an actual fact or as an ideal conception, it is the supreme type of sacrifice necessitated by love and by sin.

It is a simple historical fact that Christ's death was necessitated by sin; He suffered for sin as did all the prophets whose blood stained Jerusalem. Christ saw the threatening cloud blacken round the path He was pursuing, and He persisted in the path until in the course of nature, as we might say, the storm burst upon Him. He foresaw and deliberately met the power of sin.

But in what sense can it be said that that which is borne because of sin is at the same time borne for the remission of sin?

Self-sacrifice is not necessitated by sin only, but by love the principle of unity meeting sin : and the result, as a matter of fact, when these two principles of sin and unity meet in some actual instance, is vicarious suffering for sin, for love meets sin and bears its burden and penalty.

In ordinary life the person who vicariously bears the penalty of sin generally shares more or less in the guilt of the sin ; and is perhaps more or less unwilling to bear it ; and yet, in spite of these imperfections, the love which prompts self-sacrifice possesses a certain degree of redemptive power. Let us take one of the commonest instances of the redemptive power of self-sacrifice, and look in a perfectly dispassionate way at the case of the wife and children of a drunken man. The wife is seldom quite guiltless of fault ; she is not wholly willing to bear the consequences of his sin—yet she suffers for it and will suffer rather than leave him ; she loves him still, and fitfully and imperfectly tries to help him. Again, the children who suffer for their father's sin are not untainted with evil tendencies of the same nature ; they are not wholly innocent of needless frets, nor wholly conscious why they suffer, and they do not voluntarily do so : yet they hate the sin which makes them suffer without wholly ceasing to love their father.

We all recognise in such a case that there is a redemption in love, in innocence, and voluntary sacrifice, if the man who sins can lay hold of it.

So the prophet cried of the suffering servant, " He was despised and rejected of men . . . surely he hath borne our griefs and carried our sorrows, yet we did esteem him stricken, smitten of God, and afflicted." Through all life we tend so to esteem God's suffering servants. " Yet," he says, " he was wounded for our transgressions, he was bruised for our iniquities, the chastisement of our peace was upon him and with his stripes we are healed." And again and again we *are* healed through the wounds our friends suffer from us and the share of sorrow they bear for us.

If we recognise this principle in daily life, if we know the effect through sacrifice of even a small degree of love and innocence, we are better able to understand what would be meant by the redemptive force of the love and innocence of a soul which was perfectly at one with God, which perfectly sympathised with man, and yet perfectly hated sin—a soul which was willing to suffer to the death and to love to the end.

Then we have to ask what corresponds in our actual experience to what is technically called the "effect" of the sacrifice, the way in which it is "applied," and the conditions of receiving the "benefit" of it. Do these terms stand for realities which have any natural significance for us?

Let us first ask a simple historical question: What *have* been the benefits of Christ's death to the world—what effects, as a matter of fact, have followed from it?

In spite of the attempt made from time to time to attribute all religious intolerance, all ecclesiastical selfishness, all unprogressive conventionalism to the spirit of Christianity, it is undeniable that these are not the results of Christianity, but the forms taken in a Christian age by so much of the spirit of intolerance, selfishness, and conventionality as survives the influence of Christ, and that the whole ideal of character and conduct was revolutionised when man began to adopt the Beatitudes or the teaching of the Sermon on the Mount as an ideal of human character, instead, let us say, of the "magnificent man" of Aristotle. Other religions have indeed worked somewhat similar revolutions in the whole moral outlook; but it does not concern us here to dwell upon these. The fact that Christianity is the greatest agent of such a change is shown not only by its work among the most civilised nations of the past, but by the fact that it is to Christianity, if to any religion at all, that the most progressive races of the present look for the formation of national and individual character. The fact that professors of Christianity have now and always fallen short of their ideal, does not destroy, though it must diminish, the work that this ideal has done in the world.

But this ideal was consolidated and established by the death of Christ; it was the power of His death, as mysterious to the natural man as it is admittedly a mystery to the Christian, which converted His followers from a band of Galilean peasants into ambassadors of His kingdom: "As unknown and yet well known; as dying and, behold, we live; as chastened and not killed; as sorrowful yet alway rejoicing; as poor yet making many rich; as having nothing and yet possessing all things"; it was in the power of these splendid paradoxes that the death of their Master sent them out—that death which was, in a plain historical sense, a sacrifice on account of sin.

But plain historical facts must have a deeper significance if we are to have a philosophy of history at all; nay, if we are to see any causal power in human action and thought. What was the influence of such a death, caused as it was by love and by sin? It has an effect in the world, but how? Undoubtedly the instruments of that effect are human personalities. It is only through human thought, desire, will, action that any cause acts on human history, therefore the full effect is the direct effect, *i.e.* the effect on those who, heart and soul, enter into communion with the sacrifice.

Let us go back to the instance we took of human redemptive sacrifice—limited as it is. It is in virtue of a man's union with his wife and children that their sacrifice can avail to help him. If he is entirely hardening himself against them, their suffering may harden him more—it is "judgment" to him ; it is by his love for them, and the repentance which love works, that he can rise again from the pit into which he has fallen. They can help him in proportion as he loves and trusts them.

§ 4. This brings us to another of the fundamental religious ideas whose origin lies so far back in the early stages of the development of man that it cannot be traced with certainty—an essentially human idea which seems to have evolved independently but on similar lines among various races—the idea of communion.

It is still a disputed question whether sacrifice originated from the idea of communion, whether the two have a common origin, or whether they became amalgamated at some later period of development.

Death is not an invariable part of sacrifice, for there are meal offerings as well as animal

U

sacrifices ; and it may be questioned whether it is even the leading idea, or whether it is not still only incidental when it is, as in animal sacrifice, a necessary incident. It is urged that in this latter case the offering of the blood is the essential feature, and that the offering of the blood is not an offering of death, but the offering of life.   It is for this reason that according to the Jewish law the blood may not be eaten by the worshipper but given to the Deity, though the worshipper has rights in the dead carcase.

However this may be in sacrifice, in communion, at any rate, the prominent idea is participation in life, not in death ; and we have in the covenant of blood brotherhood an instance of communion and sacrifice without death, but accompanied by the shedding of blood, for the covenant was effected by mingling the blood drawn from the arms of the men, whereby they became of one kin.   Even where communion and sacrifice are united, the essential object of communion is communicated life. Sacrifice may be necessitated by communion, and death necessitated by sacrifice, but the death is no part of the essential object of the communion, though it may be a necessary condition of attaining that object.

The doctrines of sacrifice and communion have thus had a long history of development from ideas which we see, as we look back, are sometimes barbarous or even possibly savage. But for the full meaning of an idea we must look, not to its first manifestation but to the most complete and spiritual stage of development which we can observe. In the Christian Eucharist we have the fullest and most spiritual development of the united ideas of communion and sacrifice sacramentally realised. In the Christian Eucharist death is implied as incidentally necessary—necessary that is, in relation to the world of time and space, to the mind of the flesh which must die. But the Christian doctrine makes no halting-place at the idea of death. He who participates in the communion of the sacrifice of the death of Christ is buried *in order that* he may rise ; dies *in order that* he may live in Christ, and that the life of Christ may be made manifest in him. In this conception, dying is but the stripping off of the husk of life that the flower may bloom. Death has reference only to all the transient and evil accidents of life.

The communicant participates in the life which death set free, in a higher spiritual life than could be communicated while the Divine Personality on earth was yet individually limited. "It is expedient for you that I go away, for if I go not away the Comforter will not come unto you, but if I depart I will send him unto you." In *In Memoriam* Tennyson describes this sense of the pervading presence which is made possible by the release through death from the limitations of individuality :—

Thy voice is on the rolling air ;
  I hear thee where the waters run ;
  Thou standest in the rising sun,
And in the setting thou art fair.

What art thou then ? I cannot guess,
  But tho' I seem in star and flower
  To feel thee *some diffusive power* . . .

But the Christian Eucharist involves more
than the sacrifice of the bodily life, namely, the
sacrifice of the will : and as the sacrifice of blood
involves the death of the body, so the sacrifice of
the will involves the death of the mind of the
flesh, the destruction of the whole principle of
separation from God.

It is impossible, as the Jewish-Christian prophet
saw, that the blood of bulls and of goats should
take away sin, and remembering the sacrifice of
will made in Gethsemane and consummated on
the Cross, he quotes :—

Sacrifice and offering thou wouldest not, but a body hast
thou prepared me . . . .
  Then said I, Lo, I come to do thy will.

"by the which will," he adds, "we are sancti-
fied."

The sacramental realisation of these conceptions, which are both ideal and historical, is the
highest possible expression of the relation between
the material and the spiritual. The human mind
tries again and again to simplify the relation
between matter and spirit which it must recognise
and cannot comprehend. It tries to deny the
reality of matter and reduces all experience to

absurdity; or to deny the reality of mind and ends in a stupid materialism; for either denial robs of its meaning a relation which is involved in everything that we say, in the sacrament of language, in everything we plan and hope for, in everything which we do and are, and which is expressed nowhere more clearly than in the Christian sacrament of communion with the Divine Life.

§ 5. Thus it is clear that the idea of "propitiatory machinery" is unmeaning in connection with Christianity : there is no question of a "mechanical" transference of a commodity called righteousness, in answer to an intellectual belief or an unmoral action called "pleading Christ's death." The idea of propitiation, of a sacrifice for sin, of communion in that sacrifice, involves a number of facts connected with life and history ; of some of these the truth is manifest, but the most fundamental are as inward and as secret as life itself.

The manifest facts are those of history. In spite of all evils and all hypocrisies done under the name of Christianity, it is a manifest fact that the effect of Christ's life and teaching, consummated by His death, has been to raise the spiritual standard of the whole world; and that the chief part of the change is effected through the instrumentality of those who believe in the possibility of communion in the life of Christ.

But history can only give us facts; for the inward meaning of these facts lies in another region, the philosophy of history. And the inward meaning must be always open to question, for we touch here upon mysteries in the highest sense, that is, not arbitrary facts or simple marvels, but fundamental facts of life which must transcend our reason. The question as to what is the nature of the power which has effected the changes through human instrumentality is a question in which both reason and experience are involved; yet like other questions of the fundamental nature of anything, it must remain in some sense a mystery.

The mere fact of classifying this force with other forces, of saying for instance that the changes are worked by the force of influence, by the influence of example, does not explain anything, since we do not really understand the full meaning of "influence" and "example."

We do not even understand the mimetic changes of the lower creation, the colour changes of the chameleon or the octopus; much less do we understand what is the power through which the bird is inwardly compelled to imitate alien notes; or the higher power whereby, through conscious and unconscious impulse at once, the man whose thought and volition are centred in some adoring contemplation, is changed into the image of that on which he gazes.

We do not really explain any such phenomena

when we refer them to laws or forces of Nature ; any more than we explain some effect by saying it is due to the force of gravitation ; for laws and forces of Nature are merely the accurate summing up of certain groups of facts under some general expression.

Yet even the classification of facts is a help to further knowledge. In the instance before us the classification helps us to realise that all the effects said to be produced by influence or example are facts of a vital kind ; and that, since such influences are more or less consciously effective, if we would know the full meaning of influence we must make our observations of the highest and most spiritual influence acting on those who consciously realise it and voluntarily yield themselves to it. The experiences on which we reason must be gained in the last resort from introspection, and the highest experiences must be rare ; and we cannot set aside as fanatic the evidence given by those who know themselves open to spiritual influences, simply because these experiences are somewhat withdrawn from ordinary life ; though indeed the highest instances of spiritual experience are usually found conjoined with great intellectual and practical power.

The experiences then which are in question are vital experiences ; the "mechanical" idea can only come from separating religion as a theoretical and formal scheme from life. But the Christian belief is not a mere intellectual scheme ; it is

intimately connected with the experience of
ordinary life, and with the course of the world's
history; and it is centred in a Personality through
whom redemption from sin became a vital power
to those who immediately knew Him as well as to
men of all races who have lived and died since He
lived and died on the earth.

B. EXAMINATION OF THREE FUNDA-
MENTAL CHRISTIAN DOCTRINES
—Continued

CHAPTER IV

THE SPIRIT IN THE CHURCH

§ 1. It is strange that in spite of the growing perception of the unity of Nature there is a strong
tendency to treat religion as a purely individual
matter; to acknowledge no reality in religion
except the relation between God and the individual
soul.

This tendency is no doubt an indication of
healthy sincerity, for it recognises that if it is to
be real, man's relation to God must be intensely
and vitally individual, nothing else but the life of
his soul and the core of his existence. But this
tendency of thought becomes jejune from the
failure to recognise that man's relation to God
cannot be only an individual relation; for from
the beginning man is not individually but socially
developed; he is not cast up like a volcanic island
from the bottom of the sea. Man did not and

could not come on the scene of this world until
the cosmic order was so fully developed as to
make the supply of his material wants possible ;
he was developed from among the gregarious
creatures, and as his very existence depended on
others, so in the period of youth, uniquely long
among living creatures, his material and intellectual wants are ministered to by others. Many
living creatures are nearly ready to provide for
themselves from the moment when their individual
life begins ; the bird has some weeks, the dog
some months of protected youth, but the human
being has years of dependence. And even when
man is what we call independent, his independence is not an individual but a social independence.
He is an independent member of society, but not
a creature independent of society. His independence means that he can render back something in
return for that which he receives, but not that he
is self-sufficing. The development of the human
being simply cannot take place in isolation ; and
if man is torn out of his environment, snatched
away from social relations, condemned by force
or by accident to real solitude, that which makes
him man begins to wither away.

For what is true of the material dependence of
man is true also of his intellectual being.

The history of the deaf, dumb and blind child
Helen Keller, showing her primitive savagery while
no channel of intellectual communication was open
between her and those who supplied her material

wants, and her rapid, brilliant development when the existence of language was revealed to her, displays in a unique instance the social nature of intellectual development; while the diffusion of the same ideas throughout different countries and even contemporary discoveries of the same scientific truths, are signs of the interdependence of intellectual development.   Normally, interdependence is so universal that when we speak of the appearance of genius as a case of isolated development—a shepherd-artist, a ploughman-poet—we forget that the blossoms of genius are flowers that spring from the same root as the inconspicuous leaves which nourish the growth of the plant, and that even such flowers are not solitary, first one star then another opens when the blossoming time has come.[1]

If then in his material and mental development man is thus dependent, it is impossible to think that in his spiritual development he should be isolated, for here he is at his highest point both socially and individually.   If in the supply of his material needs we may roughly define man's object as being himself, if in his intellectual development his object is a world external to him, the object with which his spiritual life is most intimately concerned is his relation not only to God but to his fellow-men.   Therefore in this region,

---

[1] The long lines of imperishable names associated with the fifth century B.C. in Greece, with the birth of Italian painting and the Renaissance in Italy, and with the Elizabethan age in England will readily occur to the mind.

not only his existence and his development, but his object, is and must be social.

Let us take as an illustration of a study which entirely ignores this social element Professor James' *Varieties of Religious Experience* where religion is treated as if it consisted of isolated individual emotions. All that part of religion which does not consist in the immediate feeling of the individual is dealt with as if it were unreal and conventional. Sacraments are spoken of as mere rites or outward forms. But in dealing with the realities of religion it is essential to remember that the whole nature of man is social. Even the inanimate objects of the world are affected by the existence and proximity of other objects, as we recognise in such an obvious case as that of the magnet and the iron. But man above all is intimately affected, even when he believes himself to be independent, by the intellectual and spiritual condition of others ; and to treat these influences as conventional, and to regard the symbols and means of spiritual communication as mere forms, is to take a very limited view of the spiritual nature of man. To isolate the individual from his relation to the community is to revert to the old abstract method which has already proved misleading in other departments of human knowledge —in economics or political science. The isolation of a subject for purposes of study is sometimes necessary, but it becomes misleading as soon as we forget that the isolation is solely for convenience, and that the truths we are dealing with are incomplete and abstract until we have restored our subject to its context.

If man is thus essentially social, and if the spiritual man cannot be understood apart from the spiritual community, we must enquire further into the nature of the spiritual community.

§ 2. We have seen that when man begins to know the world external to him he finds that he only does so in so far as he assumes that there is a reason, a spirit of rational order in the world answering to that which is in himself; and that in the same way his action on any ethical principle presupposes a wisdom and purpose in the world corresponding to his own. Then as his spirit develops he begins to surmise that the reason and wisdom which are the basis of knowledge and purpose alike in himself and in the world without, are summed up in a spirit which without individual limitations is dwelling in the universe.

But the spirit which is thus dwelling in the universe can also, as we have seen, be apprehended by the individual consciousness in which it is immanent, and we have already determined that there is no contradiction to reason in supposing that a spirit can dwell in each member of a community and in a community as a whole.

In thinking of the historical development of this spiritual community let us try to imagine ourselves looking from without on the course of the world's development through epoch after epoch; after the nebulous mass hardened we should see life beginning to overflow the world, rising wave after wave in higher and higher forms and more vivid degrees of consciousness.

So too with other eyes we should see spiritual life rise and overflow, living upon and transforming the lower orders of life, and the end of that transformation will be the end of what we call this world.

This is the theory of the spiritual community; that there is a Spirit abroad in the world gradually through spiritual organisms, social as well as individual forms, transforming the material of this world into spiritual stuff. Each transformation can only be accomplished through a living organism; thus as the physical organism transforms chemical into vital elements and the consciousness transforms vital into intellectual elements, so the spiritual organism transforms physical and intellectual into spiritual elements. The unit of the physical organism is the single cell, but through processes of development there emerges the organised body, which consists of a multiplicity of cells, each a unit of life, but all combined in one unity of life. So the unit of the spiritual life is the individual, and yet the individuals may be combined in one unity of life inspired by the same Spirit. Such an organism is then a social organism, formed of individuals affecting and affected by one another and vitally dependent on the one Spirit through which they grow into one body.

§ 3. Let us enquire then how the Christian Church as a spiritual community with an historical existence corresponds to these dimly outlined needs and conditions of the spiritual being.

We do not need to think of the Christian Church as the only spiritual community which has existed in history; we know that spiritual men of quite other creeds have been members of spiritual communities, even as they have to some extent grasped the ideas of sacrifice or of communion; and that as the Christian Fathers themselves spoke of the "Christs" of old time, so they spoke of the "Church" of the Jews.

Again, we do not need to think of the Christian Church as outwardly one in its historical manifestation. Although we say that man as man is necessarily a member of a social community, any individual man belongs to some special race, and out of the lesser visible unities of family, tribe, and nation there is built up the ideal [1] unity of the human race.

So though we speak of the Christian Church as a historical existence, its oneness is an ideal unity which is gradually realising itself as the Church is being built up out of spiritual com-

[1] We use ideal here in its true sense of something which gradually realises itself in the course of time.

304 RATIONAL FAITH PART IV

munities, which yet can only be understood as being parts of this ideal unity. This is the explanation which St. Paul gives of the unity of the Church when he says, " In whom (Jesus Christ) each several building, fitly framed together, groweth into a holy temple in the Lord." [1]

Yet though the Christian Church is not the only spiritual community, and in one sense is not yet one community, it is the Christian Church pre-eminently which must stand as the historical existence corresponding to the theory at which we have arrived. We have already given one reason for this—namely, that for the civilised world there is no definite form of religion but Christianity which stands opposed to unreligion ; and the second reason, which is rather the inner significance of the first, is now apparent, namely, that as in the ideas of the Fatherhood of God and the Sacrifice of Christ, so in the idea of the Spiritual Community Christianity has a fulness which no other religion possesses.

The existence of the Christian Church is essentially bound up with that Personality in which the whole revelation of Christianity centres. In the first place, in respect of its origin.

It was not until that Personality had been withdrawn from the limitation of individual life that it was shed back diffusively into the world, and received not only by the individual but by the whole community from which again life radiated.

[1] Eph. ii. 21.

In this is the philosophy of Christianity as given by St. Paul and St. John; it was this return for which the disciples were told to wait. Under every form of expression Christ told them that life was coming back to them—His life. " I will not leave you comfortless ; *I* will come " ; Life from the Father—" The Spirit whom I will send unto you from the Father "—a personal Spirit, the Comforter who could not come until Jesus Himself had left them ; and yet it was the Father and the Son who would come to dwell with them and with whom they were to be one.

Even so after the birth of the Christian Church St. Paul speaks of the Spirit, the Spirit of God, the Spirit of Christ dwelling in the Christian ; of Christ being formed within, and yet of all together being formed into a perfect man, the measure of the stature of the fulness of Christ.

As the historical consequence we find the band of terrified disciples formed into the Christian Church ; we find that Church as a living principle, which, when it was dispersed by persecution, formed new centres wherever it spread, which again were cores of radiating life—persecuted in Jerusalem the Church dispersed into the world, and where its fragments fell new Churches sprang up.

But it is not only in its origin that the Church is essentially bound up with the personality of Christ, but in its sacraments of entrance and fellowship. Every material body enshrining a spirit must have observances, utterances, expressions, which are at the same time outward and inward ; every social body must have sacraments of communication.   The sacraments of the spiritual community are those material observances which signalise the special meeting-places of the divine and the human, or of human spirit in the divine ; and the great sacraments are those which are of universal import—the birth of the individual by one Spirit into one body, and the sacrament of fellowship in that one body and its transcending perennial life.   Thus the essential meaning of the sacraments lies in the Personality which is their life and their spirit.

C. CONCLUSION

CHAPTER V

THE VENTURE OF RATIONAL FAITH

§ 1. THUS the whole of our constructive argument centres on the mystery of personality.

Philosophy must make its starting-point in personality. The first philosophic attempts to discover the nature of existence through the investigation of an external world found their end in the gulf between the material and the spiritual; the great revolution effected by modern philosophy rose from the discovery that the beginning must be made by the investigation of experience itself; its aim was to find the principles which govern what the " I " thinks and feels and knows, for the " I " and its experiences are the basis of knowledge and the starting-point of philosophy.

If experience is thus the subject-matter of philosophy, we cannot contrast the external experiences as " real " with internal experiences as merely " subjective." Internal forces, moral and spiritual—love, repentance, aspiration—are not less real than experiences of chairs and tables and mountains and earthquakes. And we find if we consider our experience as a whole, not arbitrarily separating the more material and external part of the universe from the more spiritual and internal, that the underlying assumption which alone can make of our experience a coherent system of thought, is the belief in a Spirit, not ourselves, in whose ideal things are real even before they become actualised in the course of the world's history; a Spirit which makes for righteousness, in which are harmonised the contradictions of the actual and the ideal; a Spirit whose nature is love.

If we thus consider our experience as a whole we see that the principle of the spiritual world, that highest development of which we latest become conscious, echoes back through all lower experiences, so that in the material world it must find reflections of itself. Thus we can see even in the material forces of the world the *first essays*, if we may call them so, of the power of love— Love who is at last consciously known as Lord and King lies in germ in the forces that control the universe and hold the stars in their courses, whose messengers

> . . . whisper to the vast of space
> Among the worlds, that all is well.[1]

It is He who formed the bands of Orion and led forth Arcturus with his sons, the Power or

---

[1] *In Memoriam*, original version (MS.).

Spirit which has been called the Word and Wisdom of God.[1]

Corresponding to this philosophy which in different manners and varying degrees embodied itself in religious systems and myths, we find in history a series of events and a life of which the significance centres in one Personality, and the acceptance of Christianity turns on the question whether this Personality is the manifestation in history of the Eternal Idea, whether this revelation is the revelation of the actual existence of the higher, the spiritual order of things.

All our rational Christianity centres here; in this Personality we find the ultimate source of spiritual authority, the culminating redemptive sacrifice; here we find the source of spiritual life, the meaning of spiritual communion among men, and their union with the Divine.

The conclusion then of our theories is not a new theory but a Person, not a system of truths but a teacher, not a theory of suffering but a voluntary victim, not a power of life but a Spirit who is life, not a social plan for men but a Son of Man, not a theory about God but a Son of God.

The mystery of personality gathers up into itself the answer to our difficulties; but personality

---

[1] Lightfoot, commenting on Col. i. 17, says : " He is the principle of cohesion in the universe. He impresses upon creation that unity and solidarity which makes it a cosmos instead of a chaos. Thus (to take one instance) the action of gravitation, which keeps in their places things fixed and regulates the motions of things moving, is an expression of His mind."

transcends all forms of rational statement since life transcends comprehension; Christianity finds its centre not in a scheme of statements but in a Person who says, "Come unto me," "No one knoweth the Father save the Son and he to whomsoever the Son willeth to reveal him."

§ 2. Let us now look back on the difficulties which we encountered in the earlier part of our enquiry, and ask what they amount to when viewed from the constructive position we have reached.

We have realised the limitations of science; the presuppositions which it is compelled to make, the abstract nature of its subject-matter, the bounds beyond which it cannot go, and we have realised that a great part of the difficulties which science raises in relation to religion come from the attempt to transcend these limits; the determinist difficulty, for instance, results from the attempt to carry a scientific presupposition applicable to the natural world into a higher sphere, the world of moral human action, and similar difficulties are always raised when scientific forms applicable only to method of production are applied to questions of origin and purpose. Science is an abstract from reality, and difficulties must always occur if it is taken as equivalent to reality.

Again, we realised the insufficiency of historical

evidence when treated as the philosophic basis of religious belief. History cannot be the sole basis of religious belief, because the significance of history cannot be given by history itself. Again, though the similarity of other religions to Christianity is doubtless a difficulty if we divide the revelation of God to man by a hard and fast line from the discovery of God by man, the difficulty changes its aspect when we have arrived at the belief in a Word of God whose delight is in the human race, through whom all things are created, and through whom men are so made that they should seek after God if haply they may find Him, may see Him in visible things and hear His message through the Spirit.

There is an old philosophical puzzle about the race of Achilles and the tortoise, which was so run that although Achilles started only ten yards behind the tortoise and ran ten times as fast, he could never catch the tortoise up; for while he had run ten yards the tortoise had run one, and while he ran that yard the tortoise ran on one-tenth of a yard, and so it may be shown that the problem can baffle all solution by infinitesimal sub-division. Yet if Achilles ran twelve yards he would have overrun the tortoise, and thus too if we would overrun our difficulties we must fix our aim on a point ahead of them.

If we look beyond these difficulties at the mystery of personality from which we start, at the infinitude of personality which we apprehend at this point and at that in experience, but which is never wholly revealed to us, our difficulties seem to lie shrunk to smallness behind us, as we make the vast venture of faith on the evidence of things unseen and say—

> .   .   . though the darkness hide Thee,
> Though the eye of sinful man Thy glory may not see,
> .   .   . there is none beside Thee,
> Perfect in power, in love, and purity.

EPILOGUE

THUS we come back to the question from which we started : What is the rational position of the average person with regard to religious belief ? And it is clear now that the rational position will not simply mean what particular conclusions have been established by reasoning, because a rational mind ought to be in a condition of growth. If we took, so to speak, a section of a rational mind, we ought to find in it ideas in different degrees of development, from those laws of thought and the rational principles unconsciously implied in thought and action, up to ideas consciously held and rationally established; established perhaps in some one subject with expert precision.

Let us then, following the lines of the introduction, see what kind of religious belief such a rational mind would contain.

(1) The life of a fully rational person cannot be formless and aimless; it must have taken some shape, and this will imply certain principles and purposes, the recognition of certain standards, the suppression of some tendencies and the development of others. A rational life is deter-

mined by the relation to people and principles which it chooses to maintain, and this involves a more or less conscious recognition of certain ideals. These ideals imply at the least a belief in a moral world, in a spiritual power of righteousness. They may be more or less clear and conscious according to the intellectual development; and they may imply much more than this minimum of belief. The richness of their content will depend on the quality and development of the moral nature and the rational relation to the world. If the nature is deep and pure, if the experiences are wide, the relations to other persons many and varied, the spiritual needs are more sharply felt, more vividly realised. If the nature is gross, the experience barren, the relationship to others superficial, the ideals have less compelling power and a poorer content.

(2) Certain principles are implied in all our reasoning. Religion like science can only be built on optimism. As science is based on a belief in the rational nature of the world, so religious belief is based on the value of existence—that is, on some fundamental trust in Providence. The sceptic is the pessimist who cannot commit himself to a belief in the reality of order rather than chaos, in a final good rather than a final evil. It cannot be proved to us that reason and good rule the universe till the history of the universe is complete, but those who cling to this trust are those who are rational.

(3) Perhaps the largest part of our religious as of our secular beliefs are received on authority. Authority does not mean simply general consensus, but consensus of those best able to judge. In such a subject this would not mean those who were simply most logically minded, but those who were most experienced, who had the finest perceptions, those in fact who are most spiritually minded. If we are rational we shall be continually confirming our authorities, and continually assimilating that which we receive from them. In Christianity the authority is ultimately that transcending Personality, admittedly the most spiritual Personality that the world has known ; according to whose standard the authority of His interpreters is measured ; they are His interpreters in so far as in explaining and developing His teaching they not only present Him most clearly, but bring Himself nearer to us, or, more truly, bring us nearer to Him.

Further, to receive authority rationally we must be continually assimilating that which we receive. The spiritual is not the emotional ; we may receive spiritual things emotionally, but to receive them rationally we must receive them with the mind and the will ; we must act on them, we must experiment on them, we must let them permeate our consciousness.

(4) Thus our own spiritual experience is formed. We may not be able to examine these experiences with scientific exactness, dividing

accurately what we loosely call subjective and objective experiences—yet a rational mind will in the end gain through a discerning observation a great sum of knowledge about spiritual things, which it would be rash to reject because it does not admit of exact proof. We may mistake here and there; we may guess at many things we cannot know; we may have to express and even to think spiritual truths in terms which are called "dogmatic" because they are necessarily more definite than our experience can be. Yet if we rejected such knowledge as uncertain, our relation to the spiritual world would be less full, the material world would take a part disproportionately large, and our attitude would be by so much the less rational.

(5) With these results in mind, we turn back to history and find presented to us a Personality the influence of which has to be accounted for. Whether we can accept as proved all details that history gives us is another question; but it displays a life obscure in externals, yet with vast effects past and present. The significance of this has to be explained; it cannot be given by history itself, but must be interpreted by the whole religious experience of man. Thus in all religions we find echoes of this interpretation, and we meet as an objective fact in the history of Christ the life and acts, the teaching and the character which interprets and is interpreted by these universal human needs and aspirations. It is the correspondence

of the subjective and the objective which the rational mind must consider.

(6) And we cannot leave out of sight that there are many who witness to an immediate conviction of the essential truth of Christianity. There is only one kind of conviction which is really immediate, and that is the conviction of something as within ourselves. It is this immediate knowledge of a Spirit within our spirits, of a Life which is our life and yet which transcends our life, of a Will working through our will which is claimed, not as a universal nor as a permanent experience, but as an experience of transcending reality, however rare, however brief. When this is reached, what we call reasoning stops, because there is no need for it. Even when it is passed the mind says "I have known," and a rational mind which has had no such experience must remember that it is claimed by others, and consider how their claim is confirmed by their whole attitude towards the world and Man and God.

THE END

Printed by R. & R. CLARK, LIMITED, *Edinburgh.*

NEW BOOKS

LOLLARDY AND THE REFORMATION IN ENG-
LAND. An Historical Survey. By JAMES GAIRDNER, C.B.,
Hon. LL.D. Edin., Author of " The English Church in the
Sixteenth Century from the Accession of Henry VIII. to the
Death of Mary." Two Vols. 8vo. £1 : 1s. net.

EARLY CHURCH HISTORY (TO A.D. 313). By
HENRY MELVILL GWATKIN, M.A., Dixie Professor of
Ecclesiastical History in the University of Cambridge,
Author of " Selections from Early Writers Illustrative of
Church History to the Time of Constantine." Two Vols. 8vo.

THE FULNESS OF CHRIST. Three Sermons Preached
before the University of Oxford, and other Papers. By
EDWARD STUART TALBOT, D.D. and LL.D. (Cantab.), Bishop
of Southwark and Honorary Student of Christ Church.
Crown 8vo.

A COMMENTARY ON THE HOLY BIBLE. Complete
in one volume. By various writers. Edited by the Rev.
JOHN R. DUMMELOW, M.A., Queens' College, Cambridge. 8vo.

THE PERSON OF OUR LORD AND RECENT
THOUGHT. By the Rev. CHARLES FREDERICK NOLLOTH,
M.A., of Oriel College, Oxford, formerly Rector of All Saints,
Lewes. Crown 8vo.

THE RELIGION OF THE COMMON MAN. By Sir
HENRY J. WRIXON, K.C.M.G., K.C. Crown 8vo.

THE OTHER-WORLD. By the Rev. W. GARRETT HORDER.
Crown 8vo.

STUDIES : RELIGIOUS, PHILOSOPHICAL, SOCIAL,
AND CONTROVERSIAL. By FREDERIC HARRISON.
In Four Vols. Extra Crown 8vo. Volume IV. Realities
and Ideals, Social, Political, Literary, and Artistic. 7s. 6d. net.

Already Published :
Vol.　I. The Creed of a Layman ; Apologia pro Fide Mea.
7s. 6d. net.
　　II. The Philosophy of Common Sense. 7s. 6d. net.
　　III. National and Social Problems. 7s. 6d. net.

BUDDHIST ESSAYS. By Dr. PAUL DAHLKE. Translated
from the German by BHIKKHU SĪLĀCĀRA. 8vo. 10s. net.

MACMILLAN AND CO., LTD., LONDON.

BY THE LATE ARCHBISHOP BENSON

ADDRESSES ON THE ACTS OF THE APOSTLES.
With an Introduction by ADELINE, DUCHESS OF BEDFORD. Super Royal 8vo. 21s. net.

GUARDIAN.—"The book is delightful to read ; and those who do read it will certainly gain a good deal from it, not only respecting the Acts of the Apostles, but also respecting modern society and their own obligations towards it. The moral throughout is the guidance which a knowledge of the Apostolic age affords to Christian conduct at the present time, especially for those who have the responsibilities of rank, or position, or wealth."

THE APOCALYPSE. An Introductory Study of the Revelation of St. John the Divine. Being a presentment of the structure of the Book and of the fundamental principles of its interpretation. Super Royal 8vo. 8s. 6d. net.

TIMES.—"A striking and suggestive study of one of the standard difficulties of Biblical interpretation."

CYPRIAN, HIS LIFE, HIS TIMES, HIS WORK. 8vo. 21s. net.

TIMES.—"In all essential respects, in sobriety of judgment and temper, in sympathetic insight into character, in firm grasp of historical and ecclesiastical issues, in scholarship and erudition, the finished work is worthy of its subject and worthy of its author. . . . In its main outlines full of dramatic insight and force, and in its details full of the fruits of ripe learning, sound judgment, a lofty Christian temper, and a mature ecclesiastical wisdom."

ARCHBISHOP BENSON IN IRELAND. A Record of his Irish Sermons and Addresses. Edited by Rev. Dr. J. H. BERNARD. Crown 8vo. 3s. 6d.

PALL MALL GAZETTE.—"No words of mine could appreciate, or do justice to, the stately language and lofty thoughts of the late Primate ; they will appeal to every Churchman."

THE LIFE AND LETTERS OF ARCHBISHOP BENSON. By his Son, A. C. BENSON. *Abridged Edition.* Crown 8vo. 8s. 6d net.

MACMILLAN AND CO., Ltd., LONDON.